Better Homes and Gardens

ENCYCLOPEDIA
of
COOKING

Compliment-winning desserts including this Raspberry Bombe
are *Encyclopedia of Cooking* features. The origin of dishes, how-
to-do-it directions, and serving suggestions also appear.

On the cover: To get party fun and conversation off to a
good start, gather guests around a fondue pot so that each
can cook tiny Teriyaki Meatballs for the appetizer course.

BETTER HOMES AND GARDENS BOOKS
NEW YORK • DES MOINES

©Meredith Corporation, 1970. All Rights Reserved.
Printed in the United States of America.
Second Printing, 1970.
Library of Congress Catalog Card Number: 73-129 265
SBN 696-02001-7

Better Homes and Gardens

ENCYCLOPEDIA
of
COOKING

Volume 1

Every one of the Encyclopedia's 4000 recipes has been prepared and tested thoroughly in the Better Homes and Gardens
Test Kitchens by the foods editors. This group of experienced
home economists evaluates each dish on its appearance, taste
appeal, and ease of preparation. Quality standards are high
and, before selection, the merits of each recipe are considered
carefully with the homemaker's cooking enjoyment in mind.

Better Homes and Gardens Books

Editorial Director: Don Dooley

Managing Editor: Malcolm E. Robinson   *Art Director:* John Berg

Food Editor: Nancy Morton

Senior Food Editor: Joyce Trollope

Assistant Editors: Nancy Byal, Lorene Mundhenke, Sandra Wood,
Sharyl Steffens, Pat Olson

Copy Editor: Lawrence Clayton

Designers: Arthur Riser, George Meininger, Julie Zesch

Consulting Editor: Myrna Johnston

Consultant: Frederica Beinert

We are indebted to Frederica Beinert, noted food consultant and
writer. Her counsel and writing played an important role in the
initial research and development of the *Encyclopedia of Cooking*.

COOKING BY ENCYCLOPEDIA

Cooking can be fun—downright exciting, in fact—and with the right "tools," and know-how, cooking can become truly a creative adventure. The editors of Better Homes and Gardens believe that with adequate inspiration and the use of tested recipes and techniques everyone can become a good cook and turn out meals family and guests will rave about.

Now in your new Better Homes and Gardens encyclopedia the editors have put together the culmination of nearly 50 years' cooking experience. It guides you confidently through every detail of food shopping, food storing, meal planning, cooking, and serving. It even covers the building of great meals around leftovers.

No matter how many cook books you own, this encyclopedia set is designed so you can turn to it alone for the answer to virtually every cooking need. And you can rely on the tested techniques and recipes presented in your *Encyclopedia of Cooking*. The information is handy and concise. There are more than 2,600 entries and over 4,000 tested recipes. The whopping 92-page recipe index gives you ready access to each dish. Colorful, appetizing photographs and illustrations are used liberally.

Good food is not measured by the number of hours spent in the kitchen, so preparation has been streamlined without sacrificing the high quality. Often both the traditional and a shortcut version of a recipe are given.

Money-saving meals can be glamorous. You can depend upon your cooking encyclopedia to help you become a smart shopper. It tells you which foods must be used within one or two days and those which can be stored longer in refrigerator or freezer. Even while watching the budget you can select foods which are nutritious, appeal to personal likes and tastes, yet fit into the time and money you have available for food shopping.

Within these pages you will discover the regional dishes from across this great land as well as those foods which are part of other cultures or countries. With tested recipes at your fingertips there need be no hesitation about trying a dish which piques your interest. Information about each food will tell you something about its history and how it is served. You will learn how the customs and geography of many nations are reflected in the foods served both at family meals and for festival occasions.

Supermarket shelves are well stocked with fresh, frozen, and canned varieties of foods not available in the past. The herb and spice racks especially entice the homemaker who knows that superbly seasoned food is the mark of a good cook. With the cooking encyclopedia as a guide, the mysteries of seasonings unfold so that you can find out quickly which go with which foods. You'll learn how many of these seasonings have enjoyed their moment in history or have been associated with folklore.

Nutritional interest today centers on the calorie as never before. Within the *Encyclopedia of Cooking* are dishes to delight the lady who wants to stay slim or help her husband and children to eat right. The homemaker's big job of balancing the day's needs for protein, vitamins, and minerals against the calories needed by individual members of her family is simplified by the wealth of ideas.

Here the basic food groups are shown in detail with suggestions on how to combine them for a well-balanced diet. Each of the major nutrients is described in terms that make it easy to understand how they work together for good health. In addition, there is a special section devoted to tips for preparing dishes that are low in calories but memorable in flavor.

Using the right tool for the cooking job makes any task easier. With this in mind, the editors have included information on what to look for when buying pots and pans, utensils, major kitchen equipment, and small portable appliances. Outdoor barbecue equipment is covered in depth with plenty of recipes to show off skills at the grill. Chafing dish and fondue cookery are included with all the tips and techniques needed to produce elegant main dishes and spectacular flaming desserts.

Many foods have a story of their own to relate. Sometimes, as in the case of bread or nuts and berries, the history follows the growth of civilization. The food developed as man's progress in agriculture and technology evolved. Other foods are the results of extensive research to fill a need, simplify a technique, or improve product flavor or texture. Today foods with a long and colorful history may appear at the same meal with new products. This encyclopedia combines the romance of history with up-to-date information and recipes.

TABLE OF CONTENTS

A Sampling of Features in Your Encyclopedia

AFRO-AMERICAN COOKERY
Tasty "soul food" recipes you can make.

ALMENDRADO
How to make a light, airy dessert colored to match the red, white, and green Mexican flag.

ANTIPASTO
How to start your meal with a fabulous, flavorful Italian appetizer course.

APPETIZERS
Complete directory of hot and cold dips, spreads and bite-size pieces to tease the appetite and please your guests.

APPLES
How to know and buy the right apples for pies, salads, sauces, or eating. Recipes too.

ARTICHOKE
20 ways to enjoy its delicate flavor.

BARBECUE
Over-the-coals cookery with fire-building techniques, equipment tips, and good food.

BEANS
Beans plain and fancy in 12 pages. 16 recipes.

BEEF
How to buy, prepare, store, and serve all the cuts—cooking know-how too.

BERGAMOT
The herb with a role in American history.

BEVERAGES
Good things to drink and when to drink them.

BLUE CHEESE
Where it came from—ways to enjoy it.

BLENDER
Operation and care of your blender—recipes for soups, beverages, desserts, and spreads.

BOUQUET GARNI
Chef's trick for seasoning sauces and soups.

BREAD
20 pages on the staff of life with modern methods for making yeast and quick breads.

CAKE
31 great cake recipes. Cakes made with and without shortening; fancy fruitcakes.

CAKE DECORATING
Complete how-to-do-it information with step-by-step illustrations.

CANDY
Techniques—temperatures—doneness tests.

CANNING
Latest processing methods for fruits, vegetables, and meats—easy reference charts.

CASSEROLES
In-a-dish meals for family and company occasions. Also do-ahead preparation tips.

CHAFING DISH
Selection and care—how to use effectively.

CHEESE
World favorites and domestic specialties—how they are made, tips on storing, uses.

CHICKEN
Identification of types—preparation methods. 24 tasty recipes for family or guests.

CHOCOLATE
Complete cooking, baking, and drinking guide.

CHRISTMAS
Traditional foods from around the world—guest-pleasing holiday menus.

COOKIES
Bar, drop, and rolled cookies—refrigerator slices—baking, storing, and shipping tips.

CREOLE COOKERY
History, special characteristics, and "how-to" for these regional American dishes.

DESSERT
Recipes for final meal course or separate refreshment—some simple, some spectacular.

DUMPLINGS
Dumplings of all kinds for every occasion.

EASTER
Food, customs, and menus for a special day.

EGGS
Selection, nutritional value. Myriad uses of whole egg and separated white or yolk.

EQUIPMENT
How to choose the right appliance or tool for the job. Timesaving tips for use and care.

FISH
All you need to know in selecting and preparing fish—18 great recipes.

FONDUE
Beef, cheese, and dessert—recipes and how-to.

FREEZING
Preparation of food for freezing—proper wrapping materials—storage time charts.

FRUIT
Buying and storing information—appetizers, main dishes, side dishes, and desserts.

GARNISH
Planning and selection—how to make.

GROUND BEEF
Hamburger, Jiffy, and Foreign Meal Ideas.

HAM
Confusing terms explained—how cured, smoked, and marketed. Ways to serve.

HIGH ALTITUDE COOKERY
How altitude affects baked products and recipe timing—how to make adjustments.

ICE CREAM
Homemade ice creams—sodas, sundaes, and fancy desserts with packaged ice creams.

JELLY
Selection of fruit, preparation tricks. What makes jelly jell, when to add pectin.

LAMB
Delicate-flavored meat popular worldwide. **Recipes and tips on how to enjoy it.**

LEFTOVERS
How to plan ahead for flavorful leftovers—ways to stretch food dollars—how to store.

LOW-CALORIE COOKERY
How to eat well yet stay slim and trim.

MEAT
Identification of cuts by bone shapes—cooking methods—wrapping and storage tips.

MELON
How to determine ripeness—recipe ideas.

MEXICAN COOKERY
Influence of Spanish and Indian heritage. How to prepare well-known dishes.

MILK
Forms available—butterfat content—uses.

NUTS
Nuts for nutrition and flavor—how to select—how much to buy—recipe ideas.

NUTRITION
Daily requirements—how vitamins, minerals, protein, and other nutrients work together.

ORIENTAL COOKERY
Recipes and a helpful guide to the cuisine from China, Japan, and the Far East.

PEACHES
Characteristics of cling and freestone—how to judge ripeness—ways to keep color.

PEARS
Seasonal varieties—ripening techniques.

PIE
Baked and unbaked pies—fruit, custard, chiffon, ice cream, and parfait fillings.

PORK
Selecting fresh and cured pork including new lean cuts—latest cooking methods.

POTS AND PANS
How to choose the right utensil for each cooking job—ways to use for best results.

POULTRY
Birds to select—factors that influence cooking times, and methods—great recipes.

PRESERVATIVES
Hows and whys of their use in today's foods.

QUANTITY COOKERY
Preparing food for a crowd—equipment to use—recipes—safe food handling tips.

QUICK COOKERY
Menu suggestions for speedy meals—a look at time saved versus money spent.

REGIONAL COOKERY
Food favorites from around the United States.

RICE
Historical significance—types available—uses in main dishes, salads, and desserts.

ROUX
French technique for thickening of sauces.

SALAD
Menu importance with tips for tossed, molded, and arranged salads for all occasions.

SALAD DRESSING
Ways to complement a salad—preparation of cooked, dairy, and oil-base dressings.

SANDWICHES
Breads and fillings for parties, lunch boxes, and man-sized meals—how to wrap and store.

SAUCES
Secrets of smooth, well-seasoned sauces.

SCANDINAVIAN COOKERY
20 tasty recipes for foods originally enjoyed in Norway, Sweden, and Denmark.

SCRIPTURE CAKE
Ingredients gathered from Bible references.

SHELLFISH
Description of varieties available with instructions on how each is cooked and served.

SOUP
Comparison of broth, bouillon, consomme, and stock—menu uses historically and today, speedy versions, and slow-cooked favorites.

SPICE
Selection and storage—how much to use.

SQUASH
Survey of varieties—nutritive value—ways to serve raw, baked, fried, and stewed.

STRAWBERRIES
Development of cultivated varieties—how marketed—uses in salads, desserts, and jam.

STUFFING
Bread, fruit, meat, and vegetable combinations—appropriate foods to be stuffed.

TABLE SETTINGS
Types of service—choice of linens, china.

TENDERIZATION
Mechanical methods, aging, enzymatic action, and cooking—foods which benefit.

TOMATOES
History of the "love apple"—ways to serve.

TURKEY
Size to buy—forms available—how to roast.

VEAL
Selection and identification—choice of cooking method—well-known recipes.

VEGETABLES
Nutritional value—place in menu plan—basic preparation techniques—seasoning guide.

WINES AND SPIRITS
Guide to alcoholic beverages, the use of wine and liquor in cooking and cocktails.

YOGURT
History—types available—American uses.

YORKSHIRE PUDDING
What it is and how to prepare this traditional English accompaniment for roast beef.

ZABAGLIONE
Popular Italian dessert with a French cousin.

HOW TO USE
THE COOKING ENCYCLOPEDIA

Your *Encyclopedia of Cooking* is set up for your convenient and immediate use. Each 144-page volume is arranged in easy-to-follow (and easy-to-find) alphabetical order. Terms, categories and techniques are at your fingertips. And in your final volume, there is a complete Recipe Index which lists descriptively each of the nearly 4,000 tested recipes in your multi-volume *Encyclopedia of Cooking*. In short, this is the most comprehensive encyclopedia ever assembled on cooking.

Take, for example, the word orange. You can find it listed under letter O or, turn back to another volume and look under the letter C for a detailed account of Citrus Fruits. Here you find out about the whole group—the varieties, cooking characteristics, nutrition, and much, much more.

Your individual entries begin with the definition of the food, term, or category. Immediately following this is the pertinent history of the product, how it's grown or manufactured, and its nutritional value. In the case of a term or technique, how-to-do-it or what-is-accomplished information follows the historical material. And if the technique influences the nutritive value, this is indicated.

When several varieties or types of food are being considered, special treatment is given to help you broaden your knowledge of the characteristics of each type. And your encyclopedia doesn't stop there, it also gives you such information as how to judge ripeness, in what season a particular product is most plentiful, and how to wrap for storage—both for the time between purchase and preparation, and for after cooking.

Cross referencing is used extensively throughout. When additional information on a subject can be found elsewhere, the location of this material is indicated for you at the end of the entry.

Along with the terms and feature treatments relating to individual foods, your *Encyclopedia of Cooking* contains entries dealing with special categories of cookery. For example, look under Oriental Cookery and you'll discover a complete and comprehensive coverage on the special characteristics that give eye-pleasing appeal and mouth-watering flavor to the foods from our Far Eastern neighbors.

Foreign dishes are listed as individual entries, too. If you can't remember the national origin of a particular dish but can remember its name, you can look it up under its own individual entry.

Let's say you would like to prepare Tempura. Simply look under the entry "Tempura" and you'll find out exactly what it is, that it comes from Japan, and how to prepare it—along with cross references to Japanese and Oriental Cookery.

Holiday foods have not been overlooked. Menus and recipes, as well as customs, are featured under the headings of Christmas, Thanksgiving, and other special days. You'll also want to check in your Recipe Index. It expands the number of foods that you can choose by bringing together every recipe appearing in your encyclopedia which has a link to Christmas. Cookies, cakes, and other major categories are handled in the same way.

Pronunciation guides and alternate spellings are included where helpful and when both are in general usage. And if two spellings are different enough, they will fall on different pages in your encyclopedia. In cases like this, they are cross referenced to each other.

Recipes from the *Better Homes and Gardens* Test Kitchens have been selected to give you a cook book library containing nearly 4,000 recipes. Some foods, such as apples, have many menu uses. Here then, the recipes selected highlight the various ways you might serve apples. Also, special hints which make preparation easier, faster, or improve the quality of the finished dish are described and pictured throughout the feature.

Briefly then, your *Encyclopedia of Cooking* is both a set of beautifully illustrated reference books and a complete, comprehensive cook book library. The range of subjects spans all phases of cooking so that every entry contains something useful or informative for both the beginner and the expert. Finally, it makes fascinating, leisure-time reading for armchair gourmets who have a curiosity about food and a feeling for its romance. Keep it handy so that you can enjoy and use your encyclopedia regularly—and Happy Cooking!

PRONUNCIATION GUIDE

a fat, man, act
ā fate, mane, dale
ä far, father

b bat, tab, scab

ch church, much, chief

d bed, had, did

e net, pen, bless
ē me, meat, heat
ēr under, ear, mere

f off, cuff, fit

g get, trigger, hog

h he, ahead, hit
hw which, whiff, while

i pin, it, biscuit
ī fight, pine, file

j jump, junk, trudge

k cake, take, kill

l fall, call, low

m met, shim, film

n knot, son, fin
ng fling, washing, sing

o on, gloss, dog
ō note, poke, floor
ô song, nor, off
oi oil, boy, point
o͝o look, shook, boor
o͞o tool, troop, too
ou doubt, flout, out

p top, spot, snap

r deer, red, fear

s sell, glass, pass

sh dash, flash, shoe

t top, tend, hot
th thin, truth, path
ŧħ father, then, that

u sun, up, blood
uh for unaccented syllables, such as:
    a in *a*glow
    e in ag*e*nt
    i in van*i*ty
    o in wall*o*p
    u in foc*u*s

v have, liver, vat

w will, always

y yet, yarn, yak

z zebra, faze, zeal
zh mission, fission

Foreign pronunciations

French

â as the *a* in arm, alm
ä as the *e* in set, get

é as the *a* in say
è,ê as the *e* in let

i as the *ee* in see

ô as the *o* in nor
on as the *ong* in song

œ as the *e* in fertile

u as the *u* in menu

German

ä as the *a* in palm

kh as the *ch* in ach

w as the *v* in veal

Spanish

ll as the *ll* in million or as the *y* in you

ñ as the *ny* in canyon

A

ABALONE *(ab′ uh lō′ nē)* — A delectable shellfish with a clamlike flavor. It is a mollusk or marine snail with a large, muscular foot which enables it to clamp tightly onto rocky surfaces. It is this muscle that is cooked and enjoyed. Out of the shell, the muscle looks very much like a large scallop.

In North America the abalone is found only on the shores of California and Baja California. Here there are seven species of abalone of which the red and pink are most important commercially. Additional species known by other names are widely distributed off the Channel Islands, along the shores of France, South Africa, and the Pacific waters off New Zealand, Australia, and Japan.

These mollusks range in size from a few inches to nearly twelve inches across. Because the flattened shell is earlike in shape, the abalone is sometimes called the sea ear. The shell has a mother-of-pearl irridescent interior which is highly prized for use in making buttons, jewelry, and fine inlaid work.

Accompaniments

←Orange Cups, brimming with bright, crunchy cranberry-orange relish, make handsome platter companions for Ham in a Blanket.

Abalone is important both for commercial and sport fishing in California, but marketing restrictions prohibit sale of fresh abalones outside the state. However, abalone from other Pacific areas is marketed quite widely as frozen steaks. Canned and dried abalone are available in oriental specialty food shops.

Nutritional value: A 3½-ounce portion of abalone contains 98 calories. It is an excellent source of the B vitamins thiamine and riboflavin. This serving provides one-third the daily protein requirement.

How to prepare: The large abalone muscle is prepared for cooking by trimming, slicing, and pounding. Dark meat portions around the edge are trimmed away, finely minced, and used in soups, chowders, fritters, or canapés and sandwiches.

The light-colored muscle is cut across the grain in thin slices. Each slice is pounded with a wooden mallet until soft and smooth. These "steaks" are then coated with fine crumbs and sautéed very quickly in melted butter. It is important not to overcook them. (See also *Shellfish*.)

ABERTAM CHEESE—A hard cheese made from ewe's milk in the Carlsbad region of Bohemia. It is sometimes found in specialty cheese shops. (See also *Cheese*.)

ACCOMPANIMENT—An individual food or a group of special foods added to a meal to please the eye and tempt the appetite. When the tone of a meal is set by the basic menu, grace notes are added by providing well-chosen accompaniments.

Tradition plays a role in certain types of accompaniments. Custom dictates, for instance, that chutney, chopped peanuts, shredded coconut, raisins or currants, and thinly-sliced scallions are served with Indian curries. Their colors are harmonious. Their textures and tastes are in contrast to the curry flavor. (See photo on page 12.)

Accompaniments may be one or many foods at the same meal. A single golden-hued spiced peach or spiced red crab apple is eye appealing on the plate with a meat or poultry entrée. The flavor and color complement, but do not take attention from the main dish being served.

In Pennsylvania Dutch country good cooks are noted for serving seven sweets and seven sours with a meal. This wide assortment of pickles, preserves, and jellies testifies to the bounty of the local harvest and the canning and pickle-making skills of these industrious women.

Harmony and contrast in flavor, color, and texture play a part in selecting appropriate accompaniments. Creamy horseradish sauce looks attractive and tastes good with broiled beef. A horseradish and beet relish is prettier to serve with portions of white fish.

Crisp, raw vegetables give harmony of color yet contrast in both texture and temperature when served with savory stews or steaming bowls of soup. In fact, the crunchiness of celery, carrots, cauliflowerettes, or green pepper strips is a welcome addition to any meal where the menu features mashed or creamed foods, well seasoned in flavor but soft in texture.

Green beans, wax beans, carrots, beets, onions, and corn are among the many vegetables that, with the addition of herbs, spices, vinegars, or special sauces, easily convert to accompaniments. Canned or frozen vegetables are handy for this purpose. The mild flavor of fresh or canned mushrooms makes them a popular accompaniment whether served warm in a simple butter sauce or chilled in a zippy marinade.

Mustard Beans

Combine 1 cup sugar, ½ cup vinegar, 3 tablespoons prepared mustard, ½ teaspoon instant minced onion, and ¼ teaspoon salt. Bring to boil, stirring till sugar is dissolved.

Add one 16-ounce can wax beans, drained, *or* one 9-ounce package frozen wax beans, thawed. Simmer, uncovered, 5 minutes; cool. Cover; refrigerate overnight. Drain well before serving.

Pickled Carrots

      6 medium carrots, scraped and
          cut in 3-inch lengths
    ¾ cup sugar
    ¾ cup vinegar
      1 tablespoon mustard seed
    2½ inches stick cinnamon, broken
      3 whole cloves

Cook carrots in small amount of boiling salted water 5 minutes. Drain; cut in thin sticks. Combine next 3 ingredients and ¾ cup water. Tie cinnamon and cloves in cloth bag; add to vinegar mixture. Simmer 10 minutes; pour over carrots. Cool; refrigerate 8 hours or overnight. Drain before serving.

Zippy Mushrooms

    ⅔ cup tarragon vinegar
    ½ cup salad oil
      1 medium clove garlic, minced
      1 tablespoon sugar
      2 tablespoons water
    1½ teaspoons salt
        Dash freshly ground black
          pepper
        Dash bottled hot pepper sauce
      1 medium onion, sliced and sepa-
          rated in rings
      2 6-ounce cans mushroom crowns,
          drained *or* 4 cups fresh
          mushrooms, washed and
          trimmed

Combine vinegar, salad oil, garlic, sugar, water, salt, pepper, and hot pepper sauce. Add onions and mushrooms. Cover and refrigerate mixture at least 8 hours or overnight, stirring several times. Drain well before serving.

An avocado-based accompaniment of Mexican descent is delicate green in color and smooth in texture. Chili powder gives character without hotness making the Mex-ocado Sauce is a pleasant contrast to the bright corn and spicy seasonings of Summer Corn Relish. If more accompaniments are desired, add green onions, olives, and little hot peppers.

Mex-ocado Sauce

   2 ripe, medium avocados
   1 tablespoon grated onion
   1 tablespoon lemon juice
   1 teaspoon salt
   ¼ teaspoon chili powder
   ⅓ cup mayonnaise or salad
       dressing

Halve avocados and remove seeds; peel. Mash with a fork. Add onion, lemon juice, salt, and chili powder. Spread mayonnaise over mixture sealing to edges of bowl; chill. At serving time, blend in mayonnaise. Makes 1½ cups.

Summer Corn Relish

   2 cups sugar
   2 cups vinegar
  1½ teaspoons salt
  1½ teaspoons celery seed
   ½ teaspoon ground turmeric
   2 cups chopped onion
   2 cups chopped tomato
   2 cups chopped cucumber
   2 cups corn, cut from cob
   2 cups chopped cabbage

In large Dutch oven combine sugar, vinegar, salt, celery seed, and turmeric. Heat to boiling; add remaining ingredients. Cook, uncovered, 25 minutes. Stir occasionally. Pack in hot, scalded jars; seal. Makes 3 pints.

Colorful Accompaniments

Help-yourself bowls of Summer Corn Relish, Mex-ocado Sauce, and assorted finger foods tempt appetites at the buffet table.

Condiments such as mustard, catsup, and assorted bottled sauces classify as accompaniments when chosen for use with a specific food. For a more attractive table serve condiments in a pitcher or small bowl rather than placing the bottle or jar on the table. Also, heating the catsup or chili sauce before it is passed with meat is a welcome touch to assure foods enjoyed together are both served warm.

Cheeses, too, are glamorous accompaniments for a variety of foods. Cheddar cheese or one of the sliced process cheeses are first choice to serve with a fragrant apple pie or a baked fruit dessert.

Crumbled blue cheese is a pleasing topper for hamburgers or steaks right off the grill. It may be passed in a small bowl so that each diner may sprinkle on as much or as little as desired. Blue cheese also adds a sophisticated touch to a meat accompaniment when incorporated into a marinade for thinly sliced onion rings.

Cheese–Marinated Onions

        3 ounces blue cheese, crumbled
            (¾ cup)
    ½ cup salad oil
        2 tablespoons lemon juice
        1 teaspoon salt
    ½ teaspoon sugar
        Dash pepper
        Dash paprika
        4 medium onions, thinly sliced
            and separated in rings (about
            4 cups)

Combine first 7 ingredients; mix well. Pour over onion rings and chill thoroughly. Serve as meat accompaniment.

Parisians float a Parmesan-topped French bread slice in each serving of onion soup. Americans who like variety may wish to substitute shredded Cheddar cheese one time and shredded Swiss another time when serving French Onion Soup at home. The French put both bowl and bread slice under the broiler to toast the bread. An easier way is to toast the bread first, then float the crusty slice on the soup.

French Onion Soup

        4 large onions, thinly
            sliced
    ¼ cup butter or margarine
        3 10½-ounce cans condensed
            beef broth
        1 teaspoon Worcestershire sauce
    ½ teaspoon salt
        2 French or hard rolls, sliced
            and toasted
        Grated Parmesan cheese *or*
            shredded sharp natural
            Cheddar cheese

In large saucepan cook onions in butter till lightly browned, about 20 minutes. Add broth and Worcestershire sauce. Bring to boiling. Season with salt and dash pepper. Sprinkle toast generously with cheese. Place under broiler till cheese is lightly browned. Pour soup in bowls. Float a slice of cheese-topped toast atop each serving. Serves 4 to 6.

Fruit provides color as well as flavor when used as an accompaniment. Often these fruits are served hot. For example, pan-browned pineapple rings pay compliments to meats, especially pork, ham, poultry, and fish. Canned peach halves are excellent broiler mates for chops or burgers. The fruit is placed cut side up beside the meat on the broiler rack during the last five minutes of cooking. A quick brushing with melted butter or a mild barbecue sauce keeps the surface of the fruit moist and aids in browning.

Either pineapple slices or peach halves when chilled make a convenient base for a generous slice of jellied cranberry sauce or dollop of bright jelly. Should lamb be on the menu, the fruit choice may be a pear half topped with emerald-green mint jelly for the flavor accent.

With a minimum of advance preparation, oranges can be fashioned into individual fruit cups for serving cranberry-orange relish. Lemon cups are the ideal substitution for the oranges when yellow is needed as a touch of color.

A miniature scoop of tangy fruit sherbet to accompany the main course at a festive dinner is a delightful and refreshing surprise to the diners. Depending on the color scheme of the menu, select pineapple, raspberry, or one of the citrus sherbets. At certain times of the year specialty ices and sherbets such as cranberry, tangerine, watermelon, or exotic fruit flavors are available to highlight the meal.

Crunchy crackers, hot buttered toast strips, or Cheese Pastry Crisps are just right with chilled salads and equally good with hot soups. The crackers may be dressed up with poppy or sesame seed.

Cheese Pastry Crisps

      1 stick piecrust mix
    ½ cup shredded sharp process
         American cheese
      2 tablespoons cold water
         Butter or margarine, melted
         Poppy seed

Crumble piecrust stick and mix with cheese. Sprinkle water over pastry-cheese mixture, one tablespoon at a time, mixing well with fork till dough forms a ball. On lightly floured surface, roll very thin in a 12x10-inch rectangle (less than ⅛ inch thick).

Cut in 2-inch squares; brush with melted butter and sprinkle with poppy seed. Fold each square into a triangle; brush tops with melted butter and sprinkle with poppy seed. Seal edges. Bake on ungreased baking sheet at 450° about 8 minutes. Makes 3 dozen.

Seeded Crackers

Select saltines, rich round crackers, crisp rye wafers, or other crackers. Brush with melted butter or margarine. Sprinkle with onion or garlic powder, caraway seed, celery seed, dillweed, poppy seed, or sesame seed. Heat on baking sheet at 350° about 5 minutes or till the crackers are crisp and hot.

Plan the accompaniments so most preparation can be done in advance. Foods will then have time to chill, and hot accompaniments will be ready for a last few minutes' heating. (See *Appetizer, Garnish* for additional information.)

Cranberry Filled Orange Cups

Pictured as the colorful accompaniment for Ham in a Blanket on page 12—

         Oranges
      1 14-ounce jar cranberry-orange relish

Allow a single small orange for each serving *or* plan on making 2 orange cups from larger fruit. Insert the tip of a sharp knife diagonally deep into the orange. Pull out knife and make next cut at reverse angle. Continue making sawtooth cuts all the way around, watching that the points will match when they meet at the end. A deep cut to the center of the orange assures that the two parts will separate easily. (When using small oranges, cut near top of orange; for large oranges, cut in the middle.)

Loosen sections of the fruit inside orange cup so that the pieces will be easy to eat with a spoon. Top each orange cup with a spoonful of cranberry-orange relish.

Ham In A Blanket

      1 5-pound canned ham
      2 cups sifted all-purpose flour
    ½ teaspoon salt
    ½ cup butter or margarine
      3 tablespoons salad oil
      1 egg
      2 tablespoons ice water

Remove ham from can and transfer to shallow baking pan or jelly roll pan. Heat in 325° oven for 1 hour. Meanwhile, mix together flour and salt; cut in butter or margarine. Lightly beat together salad oil and egg. Blend into flour mixture. Using one tablespoonful at a time, stir in ice water till dough forms a ball. Wrap dough in waxed paper; refrigerate 1 hour.

Remove ham from oven and allow to cool slightly. Roll chilled dough to 12x16-inch rectangle about ⅛ inch thick. Wrap dough around ham, tucking edges under and trimming away excess pastry. Place ham on a baking sheet; pierce pastry with fork tines. Bake at 425° for 15 minutes. If desired, trim with pastry daisies cut from leftover pieces of the dough. Return ham to oven and continue baking until a light golden brown, about 10 to 15 minutes.

ACETIC ACID *(uh sē' tik, uh set' ik)*—A sour colorless acid which gives vinegar its characteristic sour taste and pungent odor.

ACIDOPHILUS MILK *(as' i dof' les)*—Pasteurized milk soured by the action of bacteria. The flavor and odor of acidophilus milk resemble buttermilk; however, it should not be substituted for buttermilk in recipes because of its lower acid content. A fine curd gives the milk a creamy smooth texture. The principal use for acidophilus milk is in special diets.

ACORN SQUASH—A widely-ribbed winter squash with an acorn shape. Also known as "Table Queen" or "Des Moines," the latter name indicates where it was first grown commercially. It is usually five to eight inches in length and four to five and a half in diameter. The dark green rind is thin and glossy while the orange yellow pulp is thick, tender, fairly dry, sweet, and slightly fibrous.

Nutritional value: The deep yellow flesh of the acorn squash is a rich source of vitamin A. It also contains some vitamin C and the B vitamin, riboflavin.

As intriguing to the eye as to the taste, acorn squash can be crosscut into rings for candied or glazed vegetable dishes.

How to select: Acorn squash is plentiful in late summer, fall, and winter and is most abundant during the months of October and November. For best eating quality select a squash which is firm and heavy in proportion to its size. The rind should be hard and free from cuts or bruises.

Select a glossy, dark green squash with only a few, if any, pale orange areas. A solid orange color may indicate that the acorn squash has been stored too long for retention of good quality in flavor and texture. One variety, although seen in the market infrequently, is golden-skinned when perfectly ripe. Check the variety of the squash before accepting or rejecting a particular squash because of color.

When purchasing acorn squash allow one pound for each cup of cooked squash required. Acorn squash is often baked whole or in halves. Each half makes one attractive and ample serving.

How to store: Acorn squash, classified as a winter squash, are adapted to long storage. The glossy dark green rind changes to a dull orange with some dull green coloring during storage. When storing acorn squash, keep it in a cool, dry place. Pieces of cut squash can be wrapped in a plastic bag or plastic wrap and stored in the crisper of the refrigerator.

How to prepare: The rind of acorn squash is hard and fluted making it difficult to peel. Therefore, it is easier to prepare if the rind is left on when baking, boiling, or steaming. The firm rind may then become the natural bowl for individual servings. The combination of dark green outer color with the bright yellow pulp is a colorful addition to the meal.

To prepare squash for cooking, wash the rind, scrubbing well. Cook whole either by baking or boiling, or cut in halves or quarters. Slice lengthwise with a heavy-bladed knife and scoop out the seeds and ragged fibers. Sausage, applesauce, onions, walnuts, and mushrooms are tasty fillings. Imaginative glazes may be prepared by using combinations of butter, brown sugar, liquor, and spices and herbs such as cinnamon, cloves, basil, allspice, nutmeg, and ginger.

Baked Acorn Squash

Halve and seed squash; bake cut side down in shallow pan at 350° for 35 to 40 minutes. Turn cut side up; salt. Fill if desired. Bake about 20 minutes longer or till pulp is tender. Each half makes one generous serving.

Squash and Sausage: After turning, brush each half with butter. Drizzle with 1 tablespoon honey and fill with 3 browned sausage links. Bake 25 minutes longer.

Squash and Applesauce: After turning squash brush each half with butter; sprinkle with brown sugar. Fill each with ½ cup hot applesauce. Bake 15 to 20 minutes longer.

Fruit-Filled Squash

   3 medium acorn squash
  ½ teaspoon salt
   3 cups chopped apple
   1 medium orange, peeled and diced
  ½ cup brown sugar
  ¼ cup butter or margarine, melted

Cut squash in half lengthwise; remove seeds. Place cut side down in shallow baking pan. Bake at 350° for 35 minutes. Turn cut side up; sprinkle with salt. Combine remaining ingredients; spoon mixture into squash cavities. Bake 25 minutes or till tender. Makes 6 servings.

Walnut chunks and baby onions, glistening with a cinnamon-spiced glaze, are a tempting filling for acorn squash. Glazed Squash and Onions features this flattering taste trio.

Glazed Squash with Onions

A pleasing accompaniment for pork—

> 3 medium acorn squash
> 2 cups drained, cooked tiny
>   onions
> ½ cup broken walnuts
>   • • •
> ½ cup butter or margarine, melted
> ½ cup dark corn syrup
> ¼ teaspoon ground cinnamon

Halve squash lengthwise and remove seeds. Bake cut side down in shallow baking pan at 350° for 35 to 40 minutes. Turn cut side up; sprinkle with salt. Fill halves with onions and walnuts. Combine butter, dark corn syrup, ¼ teaspoon salt, and ground cinnamon. Spoon over filling. Continue baking 15 to 20 minutes or till squash is tender, brushing occasionally with syrup to glaze. Makes 6 servings.

Stuffed Acorn Squash

A perfect side dish to include in an oven meal—

> 3 medium acorn squash
> 1 slightly beaten egg
> 1 chicken bouillon cube
> ⅓ cup boiling water
>   • • •
> ¼ cup chopped onion
> 2 tablespoons butter or margarine
> ½ cup crushed herb-seasoned
>   stuffing mix
> ½ teaspoon salt
>   Dash pepper

Cut squash in half lengthwise; remove seeds. Place cut side down on baking sheet. Bake at 400° for 30 minutes, or till tender. Scoop squash from shells (reserve shells). Mash squash; add egg. Dissolve bouillon cube in water; add to mashed squash. (Add additional water if needed to make mixture quite soft.)

In skillet cook onion in butter till tender but not brown. Stir in stuffing mix. Reserve ¼ *cup* stuffing mixture; stir remainder into mashed squash. Add salt and pepper; mix well. Fill shells (squash mixture will be thin). Sprinkle with reserved stuffing. Bake at 400° for 25 to 30 minutes or till lightly browned. Serves 6.

Acorn Elegante

> 3 medium acorn squash
> 2 cups chopped onion
> 3 tablespoons butter or margarine
> 1 6-ounce can sliced mushrooms,
>   drained
> 2 tablespoons snipped parsley
>   Salt
>   Pepper
> 1 cup shredded process American
>   cheese
> 1 tablespoon buttered cornflake
>   crumbs

Cut squash in halves lengthwise; remove seeds. Place cut side down in shallow baking pan. Bake at 350° for 35 to 40 minutes.

In skillet cook onion in butter or margarine till almost tender. Add mushrooms and parsley. Turn squash halves cut side up and season to taste with salt and pepper. Fill with onion-mushroom mixture. Bake 15 to 20 minutes or till squash is tender. Top with cheese and buttered cornflake crumbs; continue baking just till cheese melts. Makes 6 servings.

Pineapple Acorn Squash

Pineapple combined with apple makes an interesting filling for baked squash—

> 3 medium acorn squash
>   Salt
> 1 8¾-ounce can crushed pine-
>   apple, drained (¾ cup)
> 1¼ cups chopped apple
> 2 tablespoons brown sugar
> 2 tablespoons butter or margarine

Halve squash lengthwise and remove seeds. Place cut side down in shallow baking pan. Bake at 350° for 40 to 45 minutes. Turn cut side up; season to taste with salt.

Combine pineapple, apple, and sugar; fill squash cavities with fruit mixture. Dot each with butter. Return squash to oven; bake 30 minutes longer or till tender. Serves 6.

Mashed acorn squash may be prepared by scooping out the pulp after the squash has been baked, mashed, and seasoned to taste. Another method of preparing mashed squash is to cube the squash and cook covered in a small amount of boiling water for 15 minutes or till tender. Cut the rind from cubes before mashing. Season to taste. One pound of fresh acorn squash yields approximately one cup cooked and mashed.

Baked or mashed squash goes well in menus with baked ham, fried sausage, pork chops, lamb patties, and pork roast.

Nutmeg Whipped Squash

A spicy addition to a holiday meal—

>   4 cups cubed unpeeled acorn
>   squash
> ¼ cup butter or margarine
> 1 tablespoon brown sugar
> ½ teaspoon ground nutmeg

Cook squash in boiling salted water for 15 minutes, or till tender. Drain well. Cut rind from cubes. Combine squash, butter, brown sugar, nutmeg, and ½ teaspoon salt; whip till smooth. Makes 6 servings.

To freeze acorn squash, select ones that are firm and mature. Bake or boil the squash till soft. Slightly undercook to allow for reheating. Remove pulp from rind and mash. Cool completely by placing the container of squash in a pan of cold water. Stir occasionally.

Pack into freezer containers, leaving ½-inch headspace. Seal and freeze. Acorn squash should not be kept frozen longer than 12 months for maximum retention of flavor and texture.

The frozen squash should not be thawed before reheating. Place in a preheated oven and heat to the desired serving temperature. Season to taste.

Rings of acorn squash are an attractive serving variation. The rings are usually glazed or candied. To prepare rings, trim the ends from the acorn squash and discard. Slice crosswise into ¾-inch or 1-inch rings. Discard seeds and ragged fibers. Then bake or proceed with recipe directions. (See also *Squash*.)

Glazed Squash Rings

>   2 medium acorn squash
>   Salt and pepper
> ⅔ cup brown sugar
> ¼ cup butter or margarine,
>   softened

Trim ends and cut squash crosswise in 1-inch slices; discard ends and seeds. Season to taste with salt and pepper. Arrange single layer in shallow baking dish; cover and bake at 350° for 30 to 35 minutes. Combine brown sugar and butter; spread over rings. Continue baking, uncovered, for 15 to 20 minutes. Baste occasionally. Makes 6 servings.

Ham-Squash Skillet

A meal in a skillet—

>   1 pound ground cooked ham
>   1 egg
> ½ cup soft bread crumbs
> ¼ cup finely chopped onion
>   2 tablespoons prepared mustard
>   • • •
>   1 medium acorn squash
>   Salt
>   Pepper
> ½ cup brown sugar
>   2 tablespoons butter or margarine, softened

Combine ham, egg, bread crumbs, onion, and mustard; form into 5 patties. In skillet brown in hot shortening. Remove from skillet. Trim ends of squash; discard ends and seeds. Cut crosswise into 5 rings; cut each ring in half.

Place squash in skillet; season with salt and pepper. Add 2 or 3 tablespoons water. Combine sugar and butter; dot over squash. Cover; cook 15 to 20 minutes or till tender, turning once. Uncover; add meat. Cook 5 minutes longer, basting often. Makes 5 servings.

ACRID *(ak′ rid)*—A strong, unpleasant flavor or odor that is harsh and pungent. The odor, irritating fumes, and disagreeable flavor produced when fats or oils are heated above their smoking temperature is an example of acrid smell and taste.

ADE—A simple iced, nonalcoholic beverage made of fruit juice, water, and some form of sweetener. The drink is usually given the descriptive name of the fruit juice used as in lemonade.

Frozen concentrates can be purchased for lemonade and limeade, and also many other single juices and juice combinations. These commercial ades are presweetened. They need only thawing and the required amount of water added to quickly make a chilled beverage. (See also *Beverage*.)

Frosty glasses of Lemonade trimmed with mint sprigs and lemon slices are invigorating thirst-quenchers for a barbecue.

Lemonade or Limeade

    1 cup sugar
    5 cups cold water
    1 cup lemon *or* lime juice

Dissolve sugar in *1 cup* cold water and lemon or lime juice. Add remaining cold water. Serve over ice. Makes 6½ cups.

Rhubarb–Lemonade Punch

Carbonated beverage makes it bubbly—

    3 cups water
    2 12-ounce packages frozen
        rhubarb
    1 6-ounce can frozen lemonade
        concentrate
  ¼ to ½ cup sugar
        • • •
    2 7-ounce bottles lemon–lime
        carbonated beverage, chilled

In saucepan combine water, frozen rhubarb, frozen lemonade concentrate, and sugar. Cover and cook about 20 minutes or till rhubarb is very soft. Strain to remove pulp; chill liquid.

Just before serving pour rhubarb mixture over ice cubes in punch bowl. Resting bottle on rim of bowl, carefully pour in carbonated beverage. Makes 12 servings.

ADOBO *(uh dō′ bō)*—A Philippine dish containing chicken or a combination of chicken and pork. The meat is first marinated in a mixture of vinegar, soy sauce, garlic, salt, and pepper. Next it is boiled in water, then fried in pork or chicken fat.

AERATE *(âr′ āt)*—To incorporate air or carbon dioxide gas into food. Bubbles of air or gas make food light or fluffy as when egg whites are beaten, cream or gelatin whipped, or batters and doughs leavened by baking powder, soda, or yeast.

Aeration is used, too, to change or improve the flavor of some foodstuffs. For example, reconstituted frozen orange juice concentrate has more of the freshly-squeezed juice flavor when shaken up or whirled in a blender to add air.

Carbonic acid gas, formed when water is charged with carbon dioxide, is added during processing or produced naturally during fermentation to give a pleasing sparkle and bubbling taste to the aerated or carbonated beverages.

AFRO-AMERICAN COOKERY—A group of foods and dishes introduced to this country by African-Negro slaves, or which issued out of the dire economic conditions of the American-based Negro slaves. It is often confused with "soul food," although this is a fusion of African, American-Indian, European, and Creole cookery, and is not necessarily food from Africa.

In any examination of Afro-American cookery, one should bear in mind that while not all foods using the name Afro-American stem from Africa, they do have their roots in the American-based Negro slave's diet. It was he who took the "hand-me-down" foods and melded them into his traditional dishes. The difficulty is to separate the African-based foods from those which the African-Negro slave took from his new environment.

The most common Afro-American foods are gumboes from Central and East Africa; sweet potatoes and yams; bean varieties and dishes from Zanzibar, Kenya, Nigeria, and Burundi; watermelons from central Africa and Ethiopia; pigs' feet from Dahomey; rice; and possibly peanuts.

A gumbo was a staple of a black's diet. Slaves from Nigeria, Chad, Guinea, and parts of East Africa were accustomed to gumbo soups and stews. So, too, were the Zulus, Kaffirs, and Ghanese. They used okra and tomato as a base for both stews and soups. Present-day gumboes incorporate Indian ways of using herbs with Congolese methods of preparing greens. Both okra and gumbo are African words.

Chicken Gumbo

  1 **4- to 4½-pound ready-to-cook**
      stewing chicken, cut up
  4 **cups thinly sliced okra**
  1 **16-ounce can tomatoes, cut up**
 ½ **cup chopped onion**
  1 **teaspoon sugar**

Place chicken in 4½-quart Dutch oven. Add 2 cups water and ½ teaspoon salt; bring to boiling. Reduce heat; cover and simmer till *almost* tender, about 2 hours. Remove chicken, reserving broth. Cut chicken from bones; cube meat.

Skim excess fat from broth. Return cubed chicken to broth; add okra, tomatoes, onion, 2 teaspoons salt, sugar, and ⅛ teaspoon pepper. Cover and simmer about ½ hour or till okra is tender. Makes 8 servings.

In Afro-American cookery, the generous use of sweet potatoes and the deep yellow potatolike tuber yams reflects strongly the use of similar vegetables in African cookery. The yam and sweet potato were introduced to Africa by Malaysians, but historical evidence has never shown the existence of a direct relationship between the African and American varieties.

Sweet Potato Pie

Traditionally Afro-American—

  2 **large peeled, cooked, mashed**
      sweet potatoes (1½ cups) *or*
      1 18-ounce can sweet potatoes,
      well drained and mashed
 ½ **cup brown sugar**
 ½ **teaspoon salt**
 ½ **teaspoon ground cinnamon**
 ¾ **cup milk**
  2 **slightly beaten eggs**
  1 **tablespoon butter or margarine,**
      melted
      Plain Pastry for 1-crust 8-inch
      pie (See *Pastry*)

Combine sweet potatoes, brown sugar, salt, and cinnamon in bowl. Mix together milk, eggs, and butter; add to potato mixture and blend well.

Line 8-inch pie plate with pastry; crimp edges. Pour potato mixture into unbaked pastry shell. Bake at 400° for 40 to 45 minutes or till knife inserted halfway between center and edge of filling comes out clean.

Peanuts are a good example of the misnomer which is Afro-American cookery. Evidence suggests peanuts originated in

Brazil and were grown in Peru during pre-Inca days. They were probably introduced into Africa to purchase slaves. Half a ship's cargo was left in Africa as payment, half was kept on board to feed the slaves. In Africa today, peanuts are called groundnuts or goobers, names often used in this country, too.

Peanut soup is popular with Afro-Americans. It is often used with the addition of okra and tomatoes. Similar soups are enjoyed in Ghana and the Sudan. The Zulus use boiled peanuts as a vegetable; Congolese prefer them mashed as a sauce with chickens; and in Chad and the Central African Republic, peanuts or peanut butter dress squash or cooked greens. Today's Afro-American cookery specials, however, are more often than not desserts such as peanut cookies, peanut pie, or that time-honored spread.

Peanut Soup

A hearty meat, vegetable, and peanut combo warms hungry children on a chilly day—

> 1 pound cubed beef stew meat
> 1 cup chopped onion
> 1 tablespoon shortening
> 1 teaspoon salt
> 1/8 teaspoon pepper
>   Dash garlic powder
>   Dash ground nutmeg
>   Dash ground ginger
>   Dash ground cloves
>   Dash paprika
>   • • •
> 1 8-ounce can (1 cup) whole
>   tomatoes, cut up
> 1/2 cup finely chopped peanuts
> 1 6-ounce can (2/3 cup)
>   evaporated milk
> 1 teaspoon cornstarch

In 3-quart saucepan brown meat and onion in hot shortening. Add 1 1/2 cups water, salt, pepper, garlic powder, nutmeg, ginger, cloves, and paprika. Simmer, covered, till meat is tender, about 1 hour. Add tomatoes and peanuts. Blend evaporated milk with cornstarch; stir into soup. Bring mixture to boiling, stirring constantly. Makes 4 servings.

The red bean soup of Zanzibar, bean stew of Kenya, black eyed peas (cowpeas) and seafood mixtures of Nigeria, and white bean dishes of Burundi are not far removed from the bean dishes enjoyed by many Afro-Americans. Hopping John, their traditional New Year's Day dish, incorporates black-eyed peas and rice.

The African method of cooking greens also enabled Afro-Americans to provide themselves with a suitable diet. Spinach and other greens are cooked in Africa much as turnip or mustard greens, kale, and collards are cooked with salt pork or smoked pork in this country.

Salt Pork and Greens

Another time prepare this recipe using kale or collards for the greens—

> 1/2 pound salt pork
> 8 cups water
>   • • •
> 1 1/2 pounds beet, chard, turnip, or
>   mustard greens (about 16 cups)
>   Salt
>   Pepper

Cut salt pork in thin strips. Place pork and water in kettle; simmer, covered, for 45 minutes. Wash greens rinsing several times to be sure they are well cleaned. Add to pork and water. Simmer covered for 1 hour.

Drain greens, reserving liquid. Season greens and pork with salt and pepper to taste. If desired, spoon pot liquor (cooking liquid) over mixture before serving. Makes 6 servings.

Although pig's feet with tripe are used in a stew in Dahomey, use of the hog in African cooking is not extensive. Europeans introduced this animal to America, where the better cuts soon were enjoyed by upper classes. The poor were left with those parts passed over by others. Their inventiveness in using what was available enabled these less-affluent people of the South to utilize everything possible. Chitterlings, also known as chitt'lins, are hog intestines and an outstanding example of these kinds of foods.

Chitterlings

    10 pounds chitterlings
    1 red pepper, cut up
    1 clove garlic, minced

Wash chitterlings thoroughly. Trim fat leaving small amount on chitterlings for seasoning. In large saucepan cover chitterlings with water. Add red pepper, garlic, 1 tablespoon salt, and 1 tablespoon pepper. Cook until tender, about 2 to 3 hours. Drain and cut in serving-size pieces. Serve at once. Makes 6 to 8 servings.

Pan-fried Chitterlings: Dip boiled chitterlings in cornmeal. In skillet panfry chitterlings in hot shortening until brown.

Deep-Fat Fried Chitterlings: Dip boiled chitterlings in egg, then crushed saltine crackers. Fry in deep hot fat (375°) till brown.

Watermelons, native to central Africa and still growing wild in Ethiopia, were brought here either before or during the slave trade and provided a taste of "home" to the newly-arrived Africans.

Rice, too, a staple food in many African countries and well established in some of the Southern states, easily became staple food here. The South's moist, hot climate was naturally suited to its growth; thus it became readily available to people of all economic levels. For the poor, rice provided bulk and the nutrients their hard work required.

These and other numerous foods are dubbed "soul foods" by today's Afro-Americans. However, soul foods have not developed from Africans alone. American Indian and European dishes also helped establish the many food traditions. (See also *Regional Cookery.*)

AGAR, AGAR-AGAR *(ä′ gär)*—A flavorless odorless, gelatinlike substance made from seaweeds. Also called Chinese or Japanese Gelatin and Chinese or Japanese Isinglass, it is used in some oriental cooking for puddings, soups, and jellied foods.

In this country, agar is used commercially as a gelling or stabilizing agent in jellies, dairy products, and canned meats and fish. Agar also has limited use in special diet or invalid foods.

AGE—To allow to reach maturity. Many forms of foods and drinks are aged to improve flavor, color, texture, or all three.

Aging at cool temperatures improves the flavor, color, and character of wines and liquors. With time, the colors and flavors change till a peak drinking quality is achieved. For most wines, this can occur from the third to fifth year; brandies often need 15 to 20 years aging.

Natural cheeses undergo an aging process that develops the cheese variety's characteristic flavor, appearance, and texture. By varying the initial cheese preparation and the aging conditions, hundreds of different kinds of cheeses can be produced.

Meat, principally fresh beef, is aged to improve tenderness. In the traditional aging method, the meat is allowed to hang for two to six weeks under special temperature and humidity conditions. Another method speeds the aging process by using elevated temperatures. These conditions must be controlled. For this reason, meats cannot be aged in the home refrigerator. (See *Cheese, Beef, Wines and Spirits* for additional information.)

AGNEAU *(än yo′)*—The French word for lamb often used on restaurant menus.

AIOLI SAUCE *(a o′ le)*—A classic French cold sauce that is really just a highly garlic-seasoned mayonnaise. The name originates from *ail,* the French word for garlic. As many as half a dozen crushed garlic cloves are used in one cup of mayonnaise. The sauce is popular as a gourmet accompaniment for fish and seafood. (See also *French Cookery.*)

AITCHBONE *(āch′ bon′)*—An old-fashioned but still-used term for the edgebone or hipbone in meat. (See also *Meat.*)

AJINOMOTO *(ä je′ no mo′ to)* — Japanese word for monosodium glutamate often seen in recipes. (See *Monosodium Glutamate.*)

AKALA *(uh kä′ luh)*—A shrub found in the Hawaiian islands. The plant produces large, sweet berries which are red, orange, or purple in color. They look and taste much like raspberries. (See also *Berry.*)

A LA *(ä lä)*—A widely used French term that literally means "in the manner of." It is commonly used on menus in the phrase *à la carte* to indicate that the diner may order from a whole list of foods rather than ordering a set menu. Each dish has its own stated price.

When used in the name of a recipe, à la may indicate or honor the creator of the recipe as in *Torte à la Sacher,* or the country or area in which the recipe originated as in *Fruit à l'Orientale.* Use of the phrase may also mean the dish was dedicated to the person for whom it was served as in the well-known *Chicken Soup à la Reine,* puréed chicken in a creamy rich broth fit for royalty. Today *à la Reine* is also noteworthy of any dish that is both elegant and delicate.

Sometimes the use of the term is a clue to the way in which a food is cooked, especially if it is typical of a country or region. A dish labeled *à l'Aurore* has usually been cooked with a sauce in which tomato paste is used to give the dish a rosy color. *A la Grecque* alludes to a dish of Greek origin. It can also indicate that oil and lemon juices are used in preparing the food. *À la Holstein* is tacked onto Wiener Schnitzel when this Viennese-style veal cutlet is served with a fried egg on top.

Another well known use of à la is in the recipe Chicken à la King. There are many stories relating to the origin of this American recipe. Actually, it was created by a chef at the old Brighton Beach Hotel outside New York City, not for a royal personage, but for Mr. King, the owner of the hotel. It was a success from the moment it appeared on the menu.

Fancy Chicken À La King

  1 cup thinly sliced fresh
    mushrooms
¼ cup chopped green pepper

• • •

  2 tablespoons butter or margarine
  2 tablespoons all-purpose flour
¾ teaspoon salt
  2 cups light cream
  3 cups cooked chicken cut in
    pieces

  3 egg yolks
½ teaspoon paprika
¼ cup butter or margarine,
    softened
  2 tablespoons dry sherry
  1 tablespoon lemon juice
  1 teaspoon onion juice
  2 tablespoons chopped canned
    pimiento
    Buttered toast slices

In saucepan cook mushrooms and green pepper in the 2 tablespoons butter till tender but not brown. Push vegetables to one side; blend flour and salt into butter. Stir in cream; cook and stir till thick and bubbly. Add chicken and heat through, stirring occasionally.

Meanwhile, in a small bowl blend egg yolks, paprika, and the ¼ cup softened butter; set aside. To chicken mixture add wine, lemon juice, and onion juice. Have chicken mixture bubbling; add egg yolk mixture all at once, stirring till blended. Immediately remove from heat. Stir in chopped pimiento. Serve on buttered toast. Makes 6 to 8 servings.

Quick Chicken À La King

Use this version when time is pressing—

½ cup chopped onion
  2 tablespoons butter or margarine
  1 10½-ounce can condensed cream
    of mushroom soup
  1 8-ounce package cream cheese,
    softened
    Dash pepper
  2 5-ounce cans boned cooked
    chicken, diced (about 1¼
    cups)
  1 3-ounce can undrained broiled
    sliced mushrooms
¼ cup chopped green pepper
  2 tablespoons chopped canned
    pimiento
  2 tablespoons dry sherry
    Biscuits

In saucepan cook onion in butter till tender but not brown. Blend in soup, cheese, and pepper. Stir in chicken and mushrooms. Heat to boiling. Add green pepper, pimiento, and sherry. Serve over biscuits. Serves 6.

À la King has come to mean poultry, fish and shellfish, or eggs prepared and served in a fairly rich cream sauce. The sauce often includes mushrooms, bits of green pepper and pimiento, and is smoothed to velvety golden richness by the addition of egg yolks.

Eggs À La King

¼ cup butter or margarine
¼ cup all-purpose flour
¾ teaspoon salt
　 Dash white pepper
2 cups milk
2 tablespoons catsup

6 hard-cooked eggs, sliced
1 6-ounce can sliced mushrooms, drained (1 cup)
½ cup cooked or canned peas
2 tablespoons chopped canned pimiento
6 thick tomato slices
6 slices buttered toast

Melt butter in saucepan. Blend in flour, salt, and pepper. Add milk all at once; cook, stirring constantly, till thick and bubbly. Remove from heat. Stir in catsup. Add eggs, mushrooms, peas, and pimiento; heat through.

Sprinkle tomato slices lightly with salt; broil 2 to 3 minutes. Place a tomato slice on each toast slice. Spoon sauce over. Serves 6.

Prepare Fancy Chicken A La King by cooking vegetables in butter till tender. Push aside vegetables; stir in flour and salt.

Blend egg yolks and butter together before adding to creamed chicken. The egg gives delicate consistency and rich flavor.

Add cream to vegetables; stir constantly till thick and bubbly. Add chicken, wine, lemon juice, and onion juice.

When chicken mixture is hot, blend in yolk mixture. Remove from heat at once. Add pimiento. Serve on toast or in patty shells.

Another popular phrase, à la mode, is strictly defined as "in the mode or fashion." In France, the term is most often used in *Boeuf À la Mode*, a stewlike dish containing beef, vegetables, and herbs which is served with a rich brown gravy. Americans usually associate à la mode with dessert when a generous scoop of ice cream is served atop the dessert, particularly a piece of pie or cake.

Marble Squares À La Mode

    ¾ cup sugar
    ½ cup butter or margarine
   1½ teaspoons vanilla
    2 eggs
         . . .
    ⅔ cup sifted all-purpose flour
    ½ teaspoon baking powder
    ¼ teaspoon salt
    1 1-ounce square unsweetened
        chocolate, melted
      Vanilla ice cream
      Fudge Sauce

Cream sugar and butter thoroughly; stir in vanilla. Add eggs, beating just till blended. Sift together flour, baking powder, and salt. Stir into creamed mixture. Spoon *half* the mixture into another bowl; stir melted chocolate into remaining batter.

Drop chocolate mixture checkerboard fashion from tablespoon in greased 8x8x2-inch baking pan. Fill in spaces with light batter. Zigzag with spatula to marble. Do not over-mix.

Bake at 350° 25 to 30 minutes or till done; cool. Cut in squares. Top each square with a scoop of vanilla ice cream. Serve with Fudge Sauce. Makes 9 servings.

Fudge Sauce

In saucepan combine ¾ cup sugar, 3 tablespoons unsweetened cocoa powder, and dash salt. Blend in 2 tablespoons water, stirring till cocoa dissolves. Add one 6-ounce can (⅔ cup) evaporated milk; bring to boiling. Boil gently for 3 to 4 minutes till sauce thickens, stirring frequently. Remove from heat; stir in 2 tablespoons butter or margarine and 1 teaspoon vanilla. Makes 1 cup sauce. Serve warm or cold.

Feature Marble Squares À La Mode for a palate-pleasing finale. Vanilla ice cream is scooped atop thin squares of a chocolate-marbled yellow cake. Spoon thick, rich Fudge Sauce over, then watch the servings disappear. This dessert is especially suitable after a light meal. Another time serve it as the refreshment at a coffee party.

Fruit such as cantaloupe have built-in serving bowls making them ideal for à la mode desserts.

Cantaloupe À La Mode

Use luscious fresh blueberries when in season—

  ½ cup sugar
  1 tablespoon cornstarch
  1 cup blueberries
  ½ teaspoon shredded lemon peel
  1 tablespoon lemon juice
    Vanilla ice cream
  2 small cantaloupes, halved
    and seeds removed

Blend sugar, cornstarch, and dash salt in saucepan. Stir in ½ cup water. Cook, stirring constantly, till mixture boils. Add berries. Return to boiling and boil 1 minute. Add lemon peel and juice. Serve warm over scoop of ice cream in cantaloupe halves. Serves 4.

ALBACORE—A member of the tuna family. Found in Pacific waters, its weight ranges from 10 to 60 pounds. The delicate white meat is popular for top-quality canned tuna. Fresh albacore, available in markets on the Pacific coast, may be purchased whole or cut into steaks depending on the size of the fish.

The dark meat next to the backbone is oily and strong in flavor and, thus, is usually discarded in favor of the mild-flavored and more abundant white meat. This meat is very soft when raw but quickly becomes firm when exposed to heat. Poaching, broiling, and sautéing are the most frequently used cooking methods for preparing fresh albacore. (See *Fish, Tuna* for additional information.)

Buying canned tuna

Look for the words "albacore" or "white meat" on canned tuna labels if top-quality meat is desired. Albacore is the only tuna species that can be labeled "white meat."

ALBÓNDIGAS *(äl' bun dē' güs)*—A Spanish or Mexican meatball dish. The meatballs are made of either beef or a pork-veal mixture, bread crumbs, herbs, and tomato sauce then browned in olive oil. Garlic is mixed generously in the meatballs or in the sauce served over them. (See also *Mexican Cookery*.)

ALBUMEN *(al byoo' muhn)*—The transparent protein substance and major constituent of egg white other than water. (See *Egg, Protein* for additional information.)

Alcohol—A colorless, volatile, highly flammable liquid with etherlike aroma. It is produced by the action of yeasts on sugars or sugar-yielding foods such as grains, syrups, or fruits and then distilled. Only that form of alcohol known as grain or ethyl alcohol is safe to consume.

The inedible forms of alcohol have cooking uses as fuel for chafing dishes or for camp cookery. The so-called denatured alcohol used as liquid fuel or processed into solid form has been mixed with poisonous substances to make it totally unfit for drinking. *Never* bring denatured alcohol in direct contact with food or utensils that are put into the mouth. Keep it out of reach of children. (See *Chafing Dish, Wines and Spirits* for additional information.)

AL DENTE *(äl den' tā)*—An Italian phrase meaning "to the tooth." It describes the extent to which pasta products should be cooked. If a piece of cooked pasta offers just a little resistance when bitten, it is at the al dente stage. Italians say this produces the best taste and eating quality. (See also *Pasta*.)

ALE—An alcoholic beverage sometimes called English beer. It is made by fermenting barley malt and hops, but originally only malt was used. Although closely related to beer, the flavor of ale is stronger and more bitter than that of most beers. The alcoholic content of common ales usually ranges from three to five percent.

Ale is used in cooking for the preparation of some cheese dishes such as Welsh Rabbit. The beverage Ale Flip contains ale, egg, and some sugar or sugar syrup

mixed in a shaker with cracked ice. The mixture is then strained into glasses and sprinkled with nutmeg. Another use of this "beer" is in the old-fashioned hot drink called Ale Posset, a frothy, curdled combination of ale, hot milk, spices, and a little sugar. (See also *Beer*.)

ALECOST (*āl' kast*)—An old-fashioned name for the herb costmary. The word alecost dates back to the time when costmary was used as a flavoring ingredient in some types of ales. (See also *Costmary*.)

ALEWIFE—A variety of herring native to the Atlantic Ocean and found along the East Coast. This migratory fish leaves the ocean to spawn in fresh waters. Since the opening of the St. Lawrence Seaway, alewives have populated the Great Lakes.

Alewives average eight to ten inches in length and weigh about one-half pound. Most of the fish are marketed in a salt brine, although a few are smoked and an equally small number canned.

ALGAE (*al' jē*)—A mixed group of simple plants which live in fresh or salt water. A number of forms are edible. Among them are agar, dulse, and Irish moss which are useful as thickeners for some pudding-like dishes. Commercially, algae derivatives serve a variety of functions in manufactured food products, particularly as stabilizers, emulsifiers, and thickeners.

Algae frequently flavor Oriental dishes such as soups, beverages, and stews. Others find use as gelling agents. In parts of Scotland, certain forms of algae are regularly eaten as vegetables.

ALLEGRETTI FROSTING—A European term used to describe Shadow Icing, the chocolate drizzled on a frosted cake. The chocolate is allowed to drip down the sides of the cake in varying lengths, thus forming interesting icicle-like patterns. On an unusually rich cake, Shadow Icing alone may be the frosting.

Shadow Icing

In small saucepan melt one 1-ounce square unsweetened chocolate with ½ teaspoon shortening. Pour chocolate from the tip of a teaspoon in a steady stream around edge of frosted cake, letting chocolate run down sides to form "icicles" of varying lengths.

Kris Kringle Cake

A creamy white variation of allegretti frosting—

    2 2-layer size spice cake mixes
    ½ cup shortening
    1 cup boiling water
    4 eggs
    ½ cup sherry
          • • •
    7 cups mixed chopped candied
         fruits and peels
    4 cups broken walnuts
    2 cups raisins
    3 cups sifted confectioners' sugar
    3 to 6 tablespoons milk
    ¾ teaspoon vanilla

Combine cake mixes, shortening, and boiling water in large bowl. Mix till well moistened; let stand 30 minutes. Then beat at medium speed of electric mixer 2 minutes, scraping sides of bowl constantly. Add eggs and sherry; beat mixture 2 minutes longer.

Combine candied fruits and peels, nuts, and raisins; stir into cake batter. Grease one 6-inch springform pan and one 9-inch springform tube pan. Line each with heavy paper.

Pour *4 cups* batter into the 6-inch pan and remaining batter into the 9-inch pan. Bake in 300° oven 2 hours 30 minutes for small cake and 2 hours 50 minutes for large cake. Cook in pan. When cool, remove from pans. Place small layer atop large layer.

Combine confectioners' sugar and milk till of pourable but not runny consistency. Frost tops and drizzle "icicles" of varying lengths down sides. Garnish with gumdrop flowers, if desired. Makes one 7½-pound cake.

Frosting with a special look

←Gumdrop flowers and confectioners' icing used in the style of allegretti frosting dress this holiday Kris Kringle Cake.

ALLEMANDE SAUCE *(al' uh mand')*—A French white sauce. The basic ingredient is a *velouté* sauce made from the broth or stock of veal, fish, or chicken. Cream, lemon juice, nutmeg, and egg yolk for thickening are added to the *velouté*.

This golden yellow sauce is used with cooked fish, meat, eggs, and vegetables such as asparagus. Although *à l' Allemande* means "in the German style," this sauce is not German. The name refers to light color. Allemande sauce is also known as Parisienne sauce or sauce blond. (See also *Sauce*.)

Allemande Sauce

A simple way to add a gourmet touch—

2 tablespoons butter or margarine
2 tablespoons all-purpose flour
1 cup chicken broth
¼ teaspoon salt
Dash white pepper
⅓ cup light cream
1 beaten egg yolk
1 tablespoon lemon juice
Dash ground nutmeg

Melt butter in a saucepan; blend in flour. Add broth, salt, and white pepper. Cook and stir till thickened; add cream. Gradually stir about ½ *cup* of hot mixture into egg yolk; return to hot mixture. Cook and stir over low heat till thickened; remove from heat. Add lemon juice and nutmeg. Serve hot with fish, salmon, or asparagus. Makes 1⅓ cups.

ALLIGATOR PEAR—A name for the fruit, avocado. This name was inspired by its hard, thick, rough skin. (See also *Avocado*.)

ALLSPICE—A warm, sweet spice which resembles in flavor and aroma a blend of cloves, cinnamon, and nutmeg. Allspice, which is mainly produced in Jamaica, is made from the berries of the pimento tree. Spanish explorers discovered this tree with its plump brown berries in the West Indies. The fruits were mistaken for peppers; thus, they were given the name pimento, the Spanish word for pepper.

Whole allspice and ground allspice are available in the market. Ground allspice accents the flavor of vegetables such as sweet potatoes, spinach, tomatoes, squash, and pumpkin. It is often added to pies, cakes, and mincemeat. Whole allspice, resembling large smooth peppercorns, is used in pot roasts, stews, and baked hams. A hint of allspice changes an everyday food into a spicy, exciting adventure. (See also *Spice*.)

Old-Time Beef Stew

2 pounds beef chuck, cut in 1½-inch cubes
2 tablespoons shortening
1 teaspoon Worcestershire sauce
1 clove garlic
1 medium onion, sliced
1 or 2 whole bay leaves
1 tablespoon salt
1 teaspoon sugar
½ teaspoon paprika
¼ teaspoon pepper
Dash ground allspice
6 carrots, peeled and quartered
4 potatoes, peeled and quartered
1 pound small white onions
Gravy

In Dutch oven thoroughly brown meat in 2 tablespoons hot shortening, turning often. Add 2 cups hot water, Worcestershire sauce, garlic, onion, bay leaves, salt, sugar, pepper, paprika, and allspice. Cover; simmer for 1½ hours, stirring occasionally to keep from sticking.

Remove bay leaves and garlic. Add carrots, potatoes, and onions. Cover and cook 30 to 45 minutes or till vegetables are tender.

For *Gravy:* Skim fat from liquid; measure 1¾ cups liquid. Combine ¼ cup water and 2 tablespoons all-purpose flour till smooth. Stir slowly into hot liquid. Cook and stir till bubbly. Cook and stir 3 minutes. Makes 6 to 8 servings.

Festive dessert from Mexico

Airy Almendrado, studded with almonds, →
salutes the red, white, and green of the Mexican flag. (See *Almendrado* for recipe.)

ALLUMETTE *(al' yoo met')*—A French word for "match" used as a cooking and menu term to describe slivers of food cut to resemble the size and shape of a match. These slivers may be pieces of chicken, ham, cheese, vegetables, or pastry.

Most often, allumette means a thin strip of puff pastry filled or topped with a mixture such as chopped chicken livers or minced chicken, truffles, and mushrooms. The pastries are served as hors d'oeuvres.

The Swiss make a small, sweet cake which is also designated as an allumette. Puff pastry again is the base, but a sweet filling replaces the meat mixture.

ALMENDRADO—A layered Mexican dessert prepared from egg whites, sugar, almonds, and gelatin and served with an egg yolk-based custard sauce. Its name originates from the chopped almonds which are well distributed throughout. Often two layers of this fluffy dessert are tinted to coincide with the colors of the Mexican flag. Thus, the top layer is tinted green, the bottom red. The untinted middle layer remains white. (See also *Mexican Cookery.*)

Almendrado

The traditional finale for a Mexican dinner—

        1 cup sugar
        1 envelope (1 tablespoon)
            unflavored gelatin
     1¼ cups water
        5 egg whites
      ¼ teaspoon almond extract
      ½ cup chopped almonds
              • • •
        2 drops red food coloring
        2 drops green food coloring
          Custard Sauce

Combine sugar and gelatin in saucepan; add water. Stir over low heat till gelatin and sugar are dissolved. Chill till partially set; beat till fluffy. Beat egg whites with extract to stiff peaks; fold into gelatin mixture. Carefully fold in chopped almonds.

Divide mixture evenly among 3 bowls. With food coloring tint one mixture pink and another green, leaving third plain. Pour pink mixture into 8½-cup mold or 9x5x3-inch loaf pan. Next carefully layer white mixture, then green. Chill till firm. Unmold. Pass Custard Sauce. Makes 6 to 8 servings.

Custard Sauce: Combine 3 beaten egg yolks, 2 tablespoons sugar, and dash salt in medium saucepan. Stir in 1 cup milk. Cook and stir over low heat till mixture thickens and coats metal spoon; cool. Whip ½ cup whipping cream with ½ teaspoon vanilla to soft peaks. Fold into cooled sauce. Makes 2 cups.

ALMOND—The nutlike stone or kernel of the fruit of the almond tree. The delicious flavor of these nuts has been enjoyed for thousands of years. Sugar-coated almonds were distributed by the common people at such festive family occasions as marriages and births in Roman times.

Almond trees are native to the Mediterranean area and to parts of the Orient. Spanish missionaries are credited with bringing the first almond trees to America about 2,000 years ago. California provided climate in which the trees flourished.

Nutritional value: Although almonds are the source of some protein, B vitamins, and calcium, their chief role is to add flavor, texture, and eye appeal. They also add calories. Twelve to fifteen dried, unblanched almonds contain 90 calories.

Types and terms: There are two main types of almonds. Sweet almonds from pink flowering trees are the ones most generally used as salted and sugared nutmeats for out-of-hand eating or in candies, confections, baked foods, sauces, and toppings. When a recipe calls for almonds, the sweet almonds are the ones to use.

Bitter almonds from white flowering trees have a strong, distinctive flavor. Their primary use is in the processing of

A reigning beauty

Majestic is the word for a Regal Almond → Cake. No frosting is needed since sliced almonds are the crowning touch.

almond oil. These bitter almonds contain a substance which forms poisonous prussic acid and special processes are used to make bitter almond products safe to use. Some traditional European cake and cookie recipes call for the use of one or two grated bitter almonds to intensify the almond flavor. The yield of prussic acid from so few bitter almond kernels is not considered dangerous.

Many terms and names are associated with the forms in which almonds are marketed or used. The term blanched almonds refers to shelled almonds from which the brown skin has been removed.

Sometimes almonds are roasted or toasted to enhance the flavor. Roasted almonds are heated and browned in oil or butter. Roasting may be accomplished in a skillet or the oven. Toasted nuts are browned without the addition of oil.

Burnt almonds are nuts that have been toasted to a rich, dark color. They are not burned in any way. Europeans may know burnt almonds as a confection in which the almonds are covered with a crackly, very dark, candy coating.

Almonds coated with a hard sugar shell are colorful confections to be served at teas, wedding receptions, and special parties. These candy-coated nuts, known as Jordan almonds, are difficult to make at home and are generally purchased at candy or specialty food counters.

How to select: Sweet almonds come to market in many forms. Those in the shell are sold in bulk or prepackaged. The soft-shell variety can be shelled by pressure with the fingers. The hard-shell nuts require a nutcracker or hammer. In both, the nut comes out whole. Almond arithmetic is helpful in buying the right amount of almonds for recipe use. Remember that one pound of almonds in the shell equals three-fourths to one cup when shelled.

More widely used are blanched and unblanched, whole, slivered, or sliced almonds in bags or cans. Roasted almonds and unblanched, smoke-flavored almonds are also available. Dry roasted, salted, sugared, or spiced almonds are snack and confectionery foods sold in bulk, jars, or fancy canisters.

How to store: Almonds in the shell keep well for a year if stored in a cool, dry place. Shelled almonds should be stored in tightly closed containers in the refrigerator. Freezer storage is another means of keeping almonds on hand. The nutmeats should be sealed in freezer containers.

How to use: Unroasted or unblanched almonds are used in foods when the nuts or pieces will be exposed directly to the heat. Almonds to be used in salads, sprinkled atop sundaes and desserts, or salted for snacking benefit from toasting or roasting. To assure the toasted nuts stay crisp, they should be added just before the finished dish is served.

Blanched almonds are used whole, sliced, or slivered with vegetables, fish, poultry, and in fancy baking. They may be toasted or not, according to the use.

Either unblanched or blanched almonds can be chopped to desired coarseness or fineness in several ways. To chop them by hand, use a straight-edged heavy knife and chopping board. Chop only a few nuts at a time. Specially designed nut choppers make the work easier and chop the nuts without mashing. Whirling almonds in a blender produces chopped nuts, too, but pieces may not be of uniform size. If grated almonds are required, a special grater, such as a mouli, is best to use. Almonds, finely ground in a blender, may be substituted for grated if necessary.

Easy ways to blanch almonds

Blanch shelled almonds by pouring boiling water over the nuts and allowing them to stand for 3 to 5 minutes. The water is drained off and the loosened brown skin easily slips away between thumb and forefinger. Blanch small quantities at a time so that the nuts do not become soggy.

An alternate method is to cover the nuts with cold water, bring them to a boil, then drain, and slip off the brown skin.

The blanched almonds should be spread apart to dry before using in a recipe or stored, tightly covered, in the refrigerator.

Whole roasted almonds are excellent salted while hot and served as snacks. Zesty seasonings are often tossed with the nuts just before serving.

Many recipes specify slivered almonds. This is one of the popular ready-to-use forms of almonds packaged and available at the supermarket.

Almonds that have been blanched at home are easy to sliver when the nuts are moist and warm. Using a sharp knife, split the nut in half along its natural seam. Lay the pieces flat side down, on a cutting board and cut into slivers of desired width. If the nuts cool too much before they are cut, warm them in a 350° oven before continuing. (See also *Nut*.)

Creamy Chicken and Rice

Buffet pleaser with a toasted almond topper—

     ½ cup uncooked wild rice
     3 cups boiling water
     ½ cup uncooked long-grain rice
     ½ cup chopped onion
     ½ cup butter or margarine
     ¼ cup all-purpose flour
     1 6-ounce can (1⅓ cups) sliced
         mushrooms, undrained
         Chicken broth
  1½ cups light cream
     3 cups diced cooked chicken
     ¼ cup chopped canned pimiento
     ¼ cup snipped parsley
     1 teaspoon salt
         Dash pepper
     ¼ cup slivered almonds, toasted

Rinse wild rice in cold water. Add with ½ teaspoon salt to *2 cups* of the boiling water. Cook 20 minutes. Add long-grain rice, remaining 1 cup boiling water, and ½ teaspoon salt. Cook 20 minutes. Meanwhile, cook onion in butter till tender. Remove from heat. Stir in flour.

Drain mushrooms, reserving liquid. Add enough chicken broth to mushroom liquid to measure 1½ cups. Stir into flour mixture. Add cream. Cook and stir till thick and bubbly. Add rice, mushrooms, chicken, pimiento, parsley, salt, and pepper. Turn into 2-quart casserole. Top with nuts. Bake at 350° for 25 to 30 minutes. Makes 8 servings.

Regal Almond Cake

As pictured on page 35—

         Butter or margarine
     1 cup sliced almonds
     2 tablespoons sugar
              • • •
     1 cup butter or margarine
     2 cups sugar
     2 teaspoons vanilla
     ½ teaspoon almond extract
  1½ teaspoons grated lemon peel
     4 egg yolks
  3¼ cups sifted cake flour
     4 teaspoons baking powder
  1½ teaspoons salt
  1½ cups milk
     4 egg whites

Generously butter bottom, sides, and tube of 10-inch tube pan; sprinkle with sliced almonds, rotating pan till sides and bottom are evenly coated. Sprinkle 2 tablespoons sugar over almond-coated sides and bottom.

Cream together the 1 cup butter with the 2 cups sugar till light and fluffy. Add vanilla, almond extract, and lemon peel. Beat in egg yolks till light and fluffy. Sift together flour, baking powder, and salt. Add to creamed mixture alternately with milk, beating thoroughly after each addition.

Beat egg whites till stiff but not dry. Gently fold into batter. Carefully turn into prepared pan. Bake at 325° about 1 hour and 20 minutes or until cake tests done. Let cake stand in pan for about 10 minutes, then invert onto wire rack to finish cooling.

Almond Chocolate Cake

Make ahead of time—it's easy to do with a mix—

> 2 tablespoons butter, softened
> ½ cup sliced almonds
> 2 tablespoons sugar
> 1 package 2-layer-size
>   chocolate cake mix
>   Whipped cream *or* ice cream

Grease a 10-inch tube pan including center tube ¾ of the way up sides, using 2 tablespoons butter. Press sliced almonds into butter. Sprinkle with sugar.

Prepare cake mix according to package directions. Carefully spoon batter over nuts. Place baking sheet on bottom rack of oven. Bake cake at 350° about 55 to 60 minutes, or till cake tests done.

Remove from oven and cool in the pan for 10 minutes. Remove cake from pan and cool completely. Slice and serve topped with whipped cream or ice cream.

Almond Flip-Top Cake

> 2 teaspoons butter or margarine
> 1 tablespoon sugar
> ⅓ cup chopped almonds
> 1 package 1-layer-size white *or*
>   yellow cake mix
>   Orange Filling

Melt butter in an 8x8x2-inch pan; spread over bottom of pan. Sprinkle sugar over melted butter and then sprinkle with almonds. Prepare cake mix according to package directions. Carefully pour batter over nuts. Bake at 375° for 25 to 30 minutes or until cake tests done. Invert on rack and cool. Split into 2 layers and spread cooled Orange Filling between layers. Makes 9 squares.

Orange Filling: Combine ¾ cup sugar, 2 tablespoons cornstarch, and dash salt. Blend in 1 teaspoon grated orange peel, ¾ cup orange juice, and 1 tablespoon lemon juice. Cook and stir over medium heat till thick and clear. Add small amount of hot mixture to 2 beaten egg yolks. Return to remaining hot mixture; blend well. Cook and stir 2 minutes longer. Remove from heat; add 1 tablespoon butter. Cool. Makes about 1 cup.

Almond Butter Crunch

Chocolate and nuts in a delicious brittle—

> 1 cup butter or margarine
> 1⅓ cups sugar
> 1 tablespoon light corn syrup
> 1 cup *coarsely* chopped almonds,
>   toasted
> 4 4-ounce bars milk chocolate,
>   melted
> 1 cup *finely* chopped almonds,
>   toasted

In saucepan melt butter. Add sugar, 3 tablespoons water, and corn syrup. Cook, stirring often, to hard crack stage (300°). Watch temperature closely after 280°. Quickly stir in coarsely chopped nuts; spread in well-greased 13x9x2-in pan. Cool.

Turn out on waxed paper. Spread with *half* the chocolate and sprinkle with *half* the finely chopped nuts. Cover with waxed paper; invert. Spread with remaining chocolate and nuts. Chill until firm. Break into pieces.

Strawberry Satin Pie

> 1 baked 9-inch Pastry Shell
>   (*see page 39*)
> ½ cup sliced almonds, toasted
>   Creamy Satin Filling
>   (*see page 39*)
> 3 cups fresh strawberries
> ¼ cup sugar
> 2 teaspoons cornstarch
>   Few drops red food coloring
>   Whipped cream

To assemble pie: Cover bottom of cooled pastry shell with almonds. Fill with chilled Creamy Satin Filling (Picture **1**). Divide strawberries as follows: Reserve a few perfect berries for center. Crush ½ cup berries and set aside; halve remaining berries. Arrange halved and whole berries atop filling (Picture **2**).

Combine crushed berries and ½ cup water. Cook 2 minutes; sieve. Mix sugar and cornstarch; gradually stir in berry juice. Cook and stir till thick and clear. Tint with red food coloring. Cool slightly; spoon over pie (Picture **3**). Refrigerate till serving time. Top with whipped cream (Picture **4**).

To prepare pastry shell: Sift together 1½ cups sifted all-purpose flour and ½ teaspoon salt. Cut in ½ cup shortening with pastry blender till pieces are the size of small peas. Sprinkle 1 tablespoon water over part of mixture. Gently toss with fork; push to side of bowl. Repeat using 3 to 4 tablespoons more water, till all is moistened. Form into a ball.

Flatten on lightly floured surface. Roll from center to edge till ⅛ inch thick. Fit pastry loosely into 9-inch pie plate; trim 1 inch beyond edge. Fold under and crimp high. Prick bottom and sides well with fork. Bake at 450° 10 to 12 minutes. Cool.

Creamy Satin Filling

> ½ cup sugar
> 3 tablespoons cornstarch
> 3 tablespoons all-purpose flour
> ½ teaspoon salt
> 2 cups milk
> 1 slightly beaten egg
>
> • • •
>
> ½ cup whipping cream
> 1 teaspoon vanilla

Combine sugar, cornstarch, flour, and salt. Gradually stir in milk. Bring to boiling, stirring constantly. Lower heat; cook and stir till thick and bubbly. Stir a little of the hot mixture into beaten egg; return to remaining hot mixture. Bring just to a boil, stirring constantly. Cool, then chill thoroughly. Beat well. Whip cream; fold into egg mixture with vanilla.

Chicken Salad Pie

An almond-studded salad in a pastry crust—

    1 cup sifted all-purpose flour
    ⅓ cup shortening
    ⅓ cup shredded sharp process
        American cheese
    1½ cups cubed cooked chicken
    1 8¾-ounce can pineapple
        tidbits, drained (⅔ cup)
    ½ cup sliced celery
    ½ cup slivered almonds, toasted
    ¾ cup dairy sour cream
    ½ cup mayonnaise

Sift flour and ¼ teaspoon salt together; cut in shortening and ¼ *cup* cheese till pieces are size of small peas. Sprinkle 3 to 4 tablespoons cold water over, 1 tablespoon at a time, gently tossing with fork till all the mixture is moistened. Form into ball. Roll on lightly floured surface to ⅛ inch thickness. Fit into 8-inch pie plate. Bake at 450° for 8 to 10 minutes. Cool before fixing with salad mixture.

Combine chicken, pineapple, celery, and *half* the nuts. Blend together sour cream and mayonnaise. Add ⅔ *cup* sour cream mixture to chicken mixture and blend well. Spoon into pastry shell. Spread remaining sour cream mixture over. Sprinkle with remaining cheese. Chill thoroughly. Trim with remaining toasted almonds. Makes 6 servings.

Peach-Almond Ice Cream

    2 cups finely chopped peaches
    ¼ cup sugar
    1 15-ounce can (1⅓ cups)
        sweetened *condensed* milk
        Red and yellow food coloring
    1 cup whipping cream
    ⅓ cup slivered almonds, toasted

To peaches add sugar and ¼ cup water; mash. Add 1 to 2 drops *each* red and yellow food coloring. Drain; reserve juice. Add water to juice to make ¾ cup. Combine peaches, juice, and milk; pour into refrigerator trays. Freeze till firm. Break into chunks; beat fluffy with electric mixer. Whip cream. Fold whipped cream and nuts into mixture. Return to trays. Freeze firm. Makes 8 to 10 servings.

ALMOND EXTRACT—A flavoring ingredient made by dissolving the oils of sweet and/ or bitter almonds in pure alcohol. It is available on the market in various sized bottles. These bottles should be kept tightly closed during storage to prevent evaporation which can cause unpleasant strengthening of the flavor. Unless considerable baking is done in the home on a regular basis, a smaller-sized bottle will probably be the best buy. Because it can be replaced as needed, there is more assurance that the almond extract on hand will be the right strength to use.

Almond extract has many culinary uses especially with fruits such as peaches and cherries. A few drops of the extract may be added to canned pie fillings made from these fruits. Since almond extract is an ingredient in many dishes with a continental flair, it is no surprise to find it in this Quick Jubilee Sauce.

Quick Jubilee Sauce

Simplified version of cherries jubilee—serve it chilled rather than flamed—

    1 16-ounce jar dark cherry
        preserves (1⅓ cups)
    ¼ cup port
    ¼ teaspoon almond extract
        Vanilla ice cream

In small bowl thoroughly combine preserves, port, and almond extract. Chill. Serve over ice cream. Makes 1⅔ cups sauce.

Almond extract is compatible with chocolate in puddings and fillings. It also may be used alone or in combination with vanilla extract in a wide range of fancy desserts and toppings. These include delicate white cakes used for tea cakes and petits fours. The cakes may be the shortening type or an angel food.

The extract is sometimes added to intensify the almond flavor in cookies, coffee cakes, and other elegant baked foods which also contain sliced or whole almonds. The traditional Chinese Almond Cookies are a good example.

ALMONDINE *(ä muhn dēn')*—A menu term used to describe the dish in which almonds appear, usually in a simple sauce or melted butter. Amandine is an alternate spelling. (See also *Amandine*.)

ALMOND PASTE—A preparation of very finely ground, blanched, unroasted almonds, usually blended with sugar, and sometimes flavored with lemon juice, almond extract, or rosewater.

Almond paste is usually purchased ready to use, but there are versions to prepare at home. A fairly uniform paste can be made in a blender or by pounding almonds with a pestle in a mortar.

Almond paste is used in making almond macaroons, as a filling in rich coffee cakes and pastries, and in preparing the colorful marzipan confections. A layer of an almond-paste preparation through the middle and on top of the traditional British Simnel Cake is its distinguishing feature. (See *Macaroon, Marzipan, Simnel Cake* for additional information.)

Almond Horns

Takes time to make but worth every minute—

    ½ cup soft butter
    ½ cup sugar
    5 slightly beaten eggs
    2 packages active dry yeast *or*
        2 cakes compressed yeast
    ⅓ cup water
    ⅔ cup milk, scalded
    5½ to 6 cups sifted all-purpose
        flour
    ½ cup butter, firm, but not
        brittle-cold
        Almond Filling
    1 slightly beaten egg yolk
    1 tablespoon water
        Sliced almonds

Thoroughly mix the soft butter, sugar, and eggs. Soften active dry yeast in *warm* water or compressed yeast in *lukewarm* water. Cool milk to lukewarm, then stir into egg mixture along with the softened yeast. Add enough flour to make a soft dough, mixing well. Refrigerate 3 hours to chill.

On lightly floured surface, roll dough to a 14-inch square, ½ inch thick. Dot h*alf* the dough with ½ cup firm butter, then fold other half of dough over butter-dotted area; seal edges. Roll to a 20x12-inch rectangle, ¼ inch thick. Fold in thirds; seal edges.

Repeat rolling and folding of dough 3 more times, chilling after each rolling if the dough begins to soften. Refrigerate till next day or till the dough is well chilled.

Divide well-chilled dough into fourths. On lightly floured surface, roll each portion to a a 15-inch circle, ⅛ inch thick. Cut each circle into 6 wedges. Along side opposite point, spread about 1 tablespoon Almond Filling; roll up, going toward point. Place point down on greased baking sheet.

Cover; let rise in a warm place till almost double, about 30 to 45 minutes. Combine slightly beaten egg yolk with water. Brush over tops of horns; sprinkle with almonds. Bake the almond horns at 350° for 20 to 25 minutes or till done. Serve warm. Makes 2 dozen.

Almond Filling: Combine 8 ounces (1 cup) almond paste, ⅔ cup sugar, and 1 egg. Mix ingredients thoroughly.

ALMOND SOUP—A specialty of Spain and Portugal in which finely chopped blanched almonds are added to a rich, creamy chicken soup just before it is served. The almond flavor is delicate.

ALUM *(al' uhm)*—A powerfully astringent mineral salt used in food preparation to give crisp texture to certain types of pickles and maraschino cherries. The amount of alum that is allowed in commercial food processing is regulated by federal laws.

Some recipes from the past for home-canned pickles may call for small amounts of alum. This reference is omitted in most up-to-date recipes. Alum is a strong chemical, and new picklemaking techniques assure crisp pickles without it. However, homemakers wishing to use it can purchase alum at a drugstore.

When alum is used in home canning of pickles, recipe directions should be followed carefully. The amount of alum to use, the correct measure of water for dilution, and directions for rinsing after pickle soaking is completed are important.

ALUMINUM *(uh loo' muh nuhm)*— A silvery white metal, light weight, yet strong, durable, and well-suited to a wide variety of kitchen utensils. It is an excellent conductor of heat, and is second only to copper in allowing heat to spread quickly and evenly. About 1900 the first aluminum utensils were available. These were thin and lightweight; later as thick as cast iron. In 1921 a medium-weight, durable waterless cookware was introduced.

How aluminum utensils are produced: Casting and stamping (pressing) are the two basic manufacturing processes. Casting is done by pouring molten metal into a mold and then allowing the metal to harden. A utensil that is made by stamping or pressing starts with sheets of aluminum that have been rolled under great pressure to the desired thickness.

Often aluminum is used in combination with other metals for pots and pans. Because of its good conductivity, a thick layer of aluminum can be bonded to a stainless steel pan. Sometimes aluminum utensils may be lined with stainless steel to eliminate the pitting and discoloration common with aluminum.

There are several finishes applied during manufacture of aluminum—anodized, oxidized, polished, satinized, etched, hammered, spun, or pebbled. Anodizing especially resists stains and corrosion.

Some aluminum utensils are coated with attractive, colorful porcelain or synthetic enamel which is fused on the outside. And many utensils, both cast and stamped may be lined with a non-stick finish.

How to select: Each type of aluminum has its advantages and disadvantages, and it's best to keep them in mind when buying.

Stamped aluminum pans come in several thicknesses and have a smooth surface. The thinner or lighter weight the pan, the quicker it will heat. However, if the pan is too lightweight, heat will be transferred so quickly that the food may stick readily. Some very lightweight aluminum pans also tend to warp and dent.

Cast aluminum utensils are thicker and heavier than many stamped pans. Because of this, they will heat evenly and hold heat

well. Cast aluminum pans are especially good for slow cooking processes or for cooking foods with little moisture.

How to use: Aluminum will not rust but will darken, dull, and stain if foods or water containing iron or alkalies are cooked in them. Or, it may discolor when dishwasher washed. Often the stain can be removed and brightness restored when an acid food, such as tomatoes, is cooked in the pan. (This does not affect the food.) Other ways to clean pans are by scrubbing with fine steel wool pads and soap; rubbing with a cut lemon; boiling an acid solution, such as vinegar and water, in pan; or using commercial aluminum cleaners.

Avoid keeping food or hot water in a cast aluminum pan for excessively long periods because cast aluminum is more porous than stamped, making pitting a possibility.

Be sure to let lightweight aluminum baking utensils or cookie sheets cool before soaking them. Cold water striking the hot metal can cause buckling, resulting in a warped and distorted pan. Baked products will not brown evenly on warped pans.

Avoid using steel wool on aluminum pans with a highly polished or anodized finish. This will cause it to scratch the surface. Instead use whiting or silver polish. (See *Pots and Pans, Saucepans, Utensils* for additional information.)

ALUMINUM FOIL—Aluminum rolled into very thin sheets. It is shiny, easily molded, and may be used as a food wrap, pan liner, or as a cooking utensil.

Since it is both airtight and moisture-proof, aluminum foil has many storage functions. Foil of lightest gauge or least thickness is suitable for wrapping foods for refrigerator storage or for container coverings. Heavier gauge foil is best for storing foods in the freezer.

Heavy foil can be used for roasting poultry, cooking on the barbecue, or for broiling. If lining the broiler rack, be sure to cut slits to match those in the rack so that the fat will drain away. A number of types of short-time use or throw-away cooking and baking utensils are made from heavy aluminum foil. (See *Barbecue, Foil Cookery* for additional information.)

Avoid heating up the oven when the temperature soars. Cook dinner outdoors. A real adventure in eating calls for foil-wrapped Campfire Pot Roast—perfect for the barbecue grill.

Campfire Pot Roast

Brown one 4-pound beef blade pot roast for about 15 minutes on a greased grill over *hot* coals with damp hickory added. Season the meat well with salt and pepper.

Tear off 5-foot length of heavy foil; fold in half for a double thickness. Place browned meat in center. Cover meat with 6 small peeled carrots; 2 medium onions, quartered; 2 medium tomatoes, cut in wedges; and 1 medium green pepper, cut in wedges. Season vegetables generously with salt and pepper. Fold foil over and seal securely. Bake over *slow* coals 1½ to 2 hours, or till tender. Pass Tangy Barbecue Sauce. Makes 6 to 8 servings.

Tangy Barbecue Sauce

In a small saucepan combine 1 cup catsup; ⅓ cup water; ¼ cup tarragon vinegar; 2 tablespoons instant minced onion; 1 tablespoon brown sugar; 1 tablespoon mustard seed (optional); 2 tablespoons salad oil; 2 tablespoons Worcestershire sauce; 1 teaspoon dried oregano leaves, crushed; 1 teaspoon chili powder; ½ teaspoon salt; ¼ teaspoon freshly ground pepper; 1 bay leaf; 1 clove garlic, minced; and 2 or 3 drops liquid smoke.

Simmer, uncovered, for 20 to 25 minutes or till sauce is of desired consistency, stirring occasionally. Remove the bay leaf before serving. Makes 2 cups barbecue sauce.

AMANDINE (*ä′ muhn dēn′, am′ uhn dēn′*)—A French term for food served or topped with almonds. Used as a recipe term, amandine describes the use of slivered or sliced almonds as a garnish or almonds prepared with a simple sauce of melted butter or margarine. Such a garnish is used most often on cooked vegetables or fish.

Green Beans Amandine

Almonds add elegant touch to green beans—

        ¼ cup slivered almonds
        ¼ cup butter or margarine,
            melted
        1 to 2 teaspoons lemon juice
        2 cups cooked French-style green
            beans

In a small skillet cook slivered almonds in melted butter or margarine over low heat till golden, stirring occasionally. Remove from heat; add lemon juice and ¼ teaspoon salt. Heat green beans; drain. Pour hot almond sauce over beans. Makes 4 servings.

Turkey Amandine on Toast

Simple way to dress up leftovers—

        2 10¾-ounce cans chicken
            gravy
        2 cups cubed cooked turkey *or*
            chicken*
        2 tablespoons chopped canned
            pimiento
        ⅛ teaspoon poultry seasoning
        1 cup dairy sour cream
        2 tablespoons all-purpose flour
        ½ cup slivered almonds
                •   •   •
        Toast points

Combine gravy, turkey, pimiento, and poultry seasoning in a saucepan. Heat, stirring occasionally. Combine sour cream and flour; stir into turkey mixture and heat *just to boiling*. Add almonds and serve over toast points. Garnish with parsley, if desired. Serves 6 to 8.

    *Use leftover cooked turkey *or* chicken *or* a cooked boneless turkey roast.

AMBERJACK—A large amber-colored game fish found in the Gulf of Mexico, and other warm waters of the Atlantic ocean. This fish is also called amber fish. It weighs up to 100 pounds and is cut into steaks for baking or broiling. (See also *Fish*.)

AMBROSIA—Name applied to a number of types of desserts in which fruit and coconut are combined. The name ambrosia is also given to an American drink similar to a champagne cocktail or to anything with a very pleasing taste or aroma.

In the mythology of ancient Greece, ambrosia was the name given to the food and drink of the gods. It was revered as the source of their immortality. The Greeks also fed it to the horses that drew the chariot of the sun across the sky. Mere mortals who were privileged to taste ambrosia were said to have acquired increased strength, swiftness, and beauty. Unfortunately, no such spectacular promises are made to people who eat ambrosia today.

In the southern United States, ambrosia is an especially popular dessert. Some sections of the country serve it with fruitcake for the traditional Christmas dinner.

In its simplest form, ambrosia is made of sliced juicy oranges sprinkled with grated or shredded coconut, and sugar, if desired. In variations, other fruits, such as pineapple and bananas, are added for a combination of fruit flavors but oranges and coconut remain as the base.

Fresh Fruit Ambrosia

        3 large oranges
        1 fresh ripe pineapple
        1 cup shredded coconut
        ¾ cup sugar
            Dash salt

Peel oranges with a sharp knife, remove sections by cutting close to membrane. Peel, core, and dice the pineapple. Combine fruit with coconut, sugar, and salt; toss lightly. Chill for several hours. At serving time, spoon into a handsome bowl and decorate the top with additional orange sections and coconut. A few maraschino cherries and sprigs of fresh mint may be used as trimming, Makes 6 servings.

Ambrosia

Ginger ale gives slight tang to fruit mixture—

1 13½-ounce can frozen pineapple chunks, thawed
1 ripe banana, peeled
3 medium oranges, sectioned
1 cup seedless grapes *or* halved grapes, seeded
⅔ cup flaked coconut
½ cup ginger ale (optional)

Drain pineapple, reserving syrup. Slice banana on bias; dip in pineapple syrup to prevent browning. Arrange *half* of each fruit in serving bowl; top with *half* the coconut, then remaining fruit. Pour reserved pineapple syrup over. Chill thoroughly. At serving time, pour ginger ale over the fruit. Top with the remaining coconut. Makes 4 to 6 servings.

Fluffy Ambrosia

Whipped cream makes fluffy dressing—

1 16-ounce can fruit cocktail, well drained
1 fully ripe banana, peeled and sliced
1 orange, peeled and cut in sections
¼ cup broken walnuts
½ cup whipping cream, whipped
1 cup miniature marshmallows (optional)
Shredded *or* flaked coconut

Combine fruit cocktail, bananas, orange sections, nuts, and marshmallows. Fold fruit mixture into whipped cream. Chill about an hour. Spoon into dishes. Sprinkle shredded or flaked coconut over top. Makes 4 servings.

Combining oranges, pineapple, and coconut in this Fresh Fruit Ambrosia makes a delightful meal ending. Garnish with bright red maraschino cherries and sprigs of fresh mint.

AMERICAINE *(a mā' rē ken')*—A tomato-based sauce used with meat, fish, eggs, and vegetables. One of the better known recipes is Lobster à l' Americaine. The lobster is prepared with tomato, oil or butter, onion, shallots, garlic, parsley, and wine or brandy. (See also *Sauce.*)

AMMONIUM HYDROGEN CARBONATE—A leavening agent also known as baking ammonia. Ammonium hydrogen carbonate should be used only in foods such as cookies and cream puffs because an objectionable ammonia taste and odor will remain in other baked products.

ANADAMA BREAD *(an' uh dam' uh)*—A yeast bread made with cornmeal, flour, and molasses. The soft-crusted, brown bread has a pleasant aroma when freshly baked.

Traditional stories say that a New England man made the bread because his wife, Anna, wouldn't cook for him. From his exclamation, "Anna, damn her!" the recipe got its name. (See *Bread, Regional Cookery* for additional information.)

Anadama Bread

    2 packages active dry yeast
 5½ to 5¾ cups sifted all-
       purpose flour
            • • •
    ½ cup cornmeal
    2 cups boiling water
    ½ cup dark molasses
    ⅓ cup shortening
    1 tablespoon salt
    2 eggs
      Melted shortening

In large mixer bowl combine yeast and *3 cups* flour. Very gradually stir cornmeal into boiling water; add molasses, the ⅓ cup shortening, and salt. Cool to lukewarm. Combine cornmeal mixture and flour mixture; add eggs. Beat at low speed on electric mixer for ½ minute, scrape sides of bowl often. Beat 3 minutes at high speed.

By hand stir in enough remaining flour to make a soft dough. Knead on lightly floured surface until smooth (7 to 10 minutes). Place in lightly greased bowl, turning dough once. Cover; let rise till double (1½ hours).

Punch dough down; divide in half. Cover and let rest 10 minutes. Shape in loaves and place in 2 greased 8½x4½x2⅝-inch loaf pans. Cover; let double (45 to 60 minutes). Brush with melted shortening. Bake at 375° for 40 minutes. Cover with foil after 20 minutes if tops are getting too brown.

ANCHOVY *(an' chō vē)*—A tiny saltwater fish of the herring family. Anchovies are usually four to six inches in length. When fresh, the anchovy is a green color; later it turns a dark greenish blue, and then almost black. The anchovy's large mouth stretches almost to the gills. Anchovies are similar to sardines and are used in much the same way.

Native to the Mediterranean Sea and the English Channel, the anchovy has been a delicacy since the days of the ancient Romans. The best anchovies are considered to be those from the Mediterranean.

During spring and summer, anchovies are caught by the millions. Preservation methods used today were originated many centuries ago by Romans and Greeks. After being cleaned, graded, and washed, the anchovies are filleted. The fillets are then layered into small kegs and packed in a salt brine so they will age slowly.

Fresh anchovies are available only in the countries where they are caught. The anchovies which are available in American markets are preserved in salt, pickled, or packed in oil. The fillets are either packed flat or rolled around a caper.

Anchovy is a versatile food. Use it as an appetizer, a seasoning, or a garnish.

Anchovies are an ideal ingredient in appetizers. The sharp, tangy flavor whets the appetite for food and drink courses that are to follow. Fillets are popular to use in hors d'oeuvres and antipastos.

Anchovy boosts the flavor of many foods. Heighten the flavor of accompaniments by including a few anchovies. The anchovy is often used as a seasoning in soups and sauces. As an ingredient in salads, the anchovy lends flavor, texture, and color.

As a garnish, tiny anchovy fillets lend an accent of color and flavor to stuffed eggs and Wiener Schnitzel. (See *Fish, Herring* for additional information.)

Anchovy Salad

An Italian-style salad that's easy to make ahead for parties—

    1 2-ounce can anchovy fillets,
        drained
    2 large tomatoes, peeled and
        cut in thin wedges
    2 medium green peppers, cut
        in narrow strips
   12 pitted ripe olives
    8 green onions, chopped
            • • •
  ¼ cup olive *or* salad oil
    2 tablespoons vinegar
      Freshly ground black pepper
      Shredded lettuce

Separate anchovy fillets into bowl; add tomatoes, green pepper, olives, and green onions. Combine oil and vinegar and drizzle over anchovy mixture. Sprinkle with pepper. Refrigerate about 1 hour. At serving time spoon over shredded lettuce. Makes 4 servings.

Italian Green Salad

    1 head romaine
    1 bunch leaf lettuce
    2 tomatoes, cut in wedges
  ½ cup sliced celery
  ½ cup diced green pepper
  ½ cup sliced radishes
  ¼ cup sliced green onion
    1 2-ounce can anchovy fillets,
        drained and chopped
            • • •
    3 tablespoons olive *or* salad oil
    2 tablespoons tarragon vinegar
    2 tablespoons chopped parsley
  ¾ teaspoon salt
  ½ teaspoon whole basil leaves
      Dash freshly ground black
        pepper

Tear romaine and leaf lettuce into bite-size pieces in salad bowl; arrange tomatoes, celery, green pepper, radishes, green onion, and anchovies over lettuce. Combine olive oil, vinegar, parsley, salt, basil, and pepper in screw top jar; shake well. Sprinkle over salad; toss lightly. Makes 6 to 8 servings.

ANCHOVY PASTE—Boned anchovies that are pounded and blended into a paste. A small amount of anchovy paste gives a great deal of flavor. Use the paste sparingly; start with approximately ⅛ teaspoon per cup of food. Taste before adding more.

Anchovy paste is used to garnish fish, eggs, and appetizers. As an ingredient, anchovy paste turns a bland dish into one that is salty and rich-flavored. Add zip to soups, mayonnaise, butter, and sauces such as white sauce with anchovy paste. A broiled steak spread with a blend of anchovy and butter is delicious.

Anchovy paste is a good item to keep on the kitchen supply shelf. Leftover foods can be transformed into sharp new dishes with the addition of this paste. If unexpected guests arrive, serve quick but elegant canapés and appetizers by combining dips, spreads, or other available foods with a small amount of anchovy paste.

Anchovy Butter Sauce

  ¼ cup butter or margarine
    1 tablespoon snipped parsley
    1 tablespoon lemon juice
    2 teaspoons anchovy paste
  ½ teaspoon prepared mustard
  ¼ teaspoon sugar

Melt butter; add remaining ingredients and stir till well blended. Serve hot with broiled fish. Makes about ⅓ cup sauce.

Anchovy Dip

    1 8-ounce package cream cheese,
        softened
    1 tablespoon anchovy paste
    1 tablespoon snipped green onion
        tops
    2 tablespoons chopped pimiento-
        stuffed green olives
    1 teaspoon lemon juice
  ¼ teaspoon Worcestershire sauce
    1 tablespoon milk

Combine all ingredients in small mixer bowl. Beat at medium speed on electric mixer till light and fluffy. Chill. Makes 2 cups.

ANGEL FOOD CAKE—A white foam cake made by combining stiffly beaten egg whites, sugar, flour, and cream of tartar. No shortening is used. Soft, white, and light as a feather from an angel's wing is one way to describe this delicate cake. Success of such a grandiose nature depends on the way in which the ingredients are prepared and blended together as well as the way in which the cake is baked.

Egg white, the basic ingredient, functions as the sole leavening agent. Allow the whites to reach room temperature before they are beaten. Slightly warm egg whites can be whipped to a greater volume than cold ones from the refrigerator.

In angel cake preparation, the whites are whipped to the stiff peak stage so that numerous small air bubbles will be held in the foam. As the cake bakes, the moisture within each bubble turns to steam causing it to expand. Up to a point, the smaller the bubbles produced when the egg whites are whipped, the finer the resulting texture.

The importance of well-beaten egg whites cannot be overemphasized. Perfectly beaten egg whites stand in stiff peaks when the beaters are slowly withdrawn, are moist and glossy, and do not slide out of the bowl when it is tipped. Not enough air bubbles are formed when the whites are underbeaten. The walls of the egg white cells will not be thin and elastic enough to give the cake good volume and texture. Overbeating also produces a small cake, but in this case the cell walls break during beating and the cake doesn't rise.

When egg whites are beaten with a fine wire whip, the angel cake usually has greater volume; but the texture will generally be coarser with relatively large holes. Using hand or electric beaters produces a finer-grained cake having slightly less, yet perfectly acceptable, volume.

Sugar serves several functions in preparation as well as in the final product structure. In most angel cake recipes, the sugar is added in two parts. The portion beaten into the egg whites increases whipping time but reduces the possibility of overwhipping. Sugar also helps to make a fine foam that will hold up for mixing with dry ingredients. The portion mixed with the flour separates the flour granules. This lessens the chance of clumps when the flour is folded into the egg whites.

In the baked angel food cake, sugar adds sweetness to the flavor. A high proportion of sugar also produces a very tender cake; but if too high, the excessive amount of sugar will cause the cake to fall.

Because fine granulated sugar, such as superfine, dissolves more readily, it is often preferred for making angel food cake. Confectioners' sugar is sometimes recommended to give the cake a special melt-in-the-mouth quality that many people desire.

Cake flour is used in preference to all-purpose flour for a tender, delicate crumb and for good cake volume. The proper proportion of flour is essential as too much flour increases toughness.

The small amount of cream of tartar involved performs two important roles in the angel cake batter. It increases the stability of the egg white foam and gives the cake crumb a bleached whiteness.

How to prepare: All angel cakes are prepared in a fairly similar manner. Before starting, check carefully to see that all utensils are free of any fat. Egg whites will not whip when fat is present.

The egg whites are beaten till foamy. Salt, cream of tartar, and flavorings are then added. A portion of sugar is added, and the mixture beaten till stiff peaks form.

Cake flour is sifted twice with the remaining sugar. The flour mixture is added to the egg white mixture in three or four portions. A down-up-and-over folding motion gently blends ingredients together. Folding should stop just as soon as blending is complete as continued folding will tend to toughen the angel cake.

An ungreased pan, traditionally tube shaped, is used to allow the batter to cling to the sides of the pan as it rises during baking. Baking temperatures and times have been determined through much

A flattering complement

← Angel Cake, topped with whipped cream and strawberries, brings welcome praises when that homemade cake goodness is recognized.

testing, and recipe directions should be followed carefully. The higher oven temperatures (375° to 400°) produce a product with greater tenderness, more moistness, and better volume than angel food cakes baked at lower temperatures.

Bake till the cake just shrinks slightly from the sides of the pan, is a delicate brown, and springs back when the surface is lightly touched with the finger. Overbaking toughens while underbaking causes the cake to shrink and fall out of the pan during the cooling period.

Angel cake should always be thoroughly cooled in an upside-down position before being removed from the pan. This allows the light structure to firm up. If removed too early, the cake will collapse. A tube pan can easily be hung for cooling with the tube set on an inverted funnel or on the neck of a sturdy bottle.

A perfect angel food cake is light brown outside and white inside. The crust is tender but not sticky, the top evenly rounded. The crumb is tender, moist, velvety, with fine, even holes and a delicate flavor. It's easy to make by following directions exactly and a joy to serve with justifiable pride.

Angel Cake

Unequaled in delicateness—

>   1 cup sifted cake flour
>   ¾ cup sugar
>   1½ cups (12) egg whites
>   1½ teaspoons cream of tartar
>   1½ teaspoons vanilla
>   ¼ teaspoon salt
>   ¾ cup sugar

Sift flour with the first ¾ cup sugar 2 times; set aside. Beat egg whites till foamy. Add cream of tartar, vanilla, and salt; continue beating till stiff enough to form soft peaks but still moist and glossy. Add remaining ¾ cup sugar, 2 tablespoons at a time, continuing to beat till egg whites hold stiff peaks.

Sift about a *fourth* of the flour mixture over whites; fold in. Repeat, folding in remaining flour by fourths. Bake in *ungreased* 10-inch tube pan at 375° for 35 to 40 minutes or till done. Invert cake in pan; cool thoroughly.

The homemaker can create infinite variations starting with basic Angel Cake. Introduce flavors such as rum, almond, lemon, peppermint, or cinnamon through the addition of flavorings and spices. Finely chopped nuts or candied fruits add crunchy texture nicely. Chocolate Angel Cake evolves from incorporation of cocoa powder in the flour mixture.

Baked angel cakes can be the bases for variations with a different theme. Fluffy fillings yield matchless taste-tempting desserts such as Raspberry Angel Dessert.

Chocolate Angel Cake

Prepare Angel Cake by substituting ¾ cup sifted cake flour and ¼ cup unsweetened cocoa powder for 1 cup sifted cake flour. Sift cocoa with flour and sugar 2 times.

Raspberry Angel Dessert

>   1 10-inch tube angel food cake
>   ½ cup sugar
>   ⅓ cup all-purpose flour
>   2 cups milk
>   3 slightly beaten egg yolks
>   1 teaspoon vanilla
>   1 cup whipping cream, whipped
>   Sweetened raspberries

Slice cake in 3 layers. Prepare filling by mixing sugar, flour, and ½ teaspoon salt in saucepan. Slowly add milk; mix well. Cook and stir over medium heat till mixture is thick and bubbly; cook 2 minutes more.

Stir some of hot mixture into egg yolks; return to hot mixture. Bring just to boiling, stirring constantly. Remove from heat; add vanilla. Cool. Fold whipped cream into pudding. Reassemble cake, spreading filling between layers and on top. Garnish with raspberries and, if desired, fresh mint leaves.

A heavenly dessert

Crowned with fresh red raspberries and mint →
leaves, Raspberry Angel Dessert boasts of a rich creamy flavor with billowy lightness.

No hard-nosed rule dictates the type of pan in which angel food cake is baked although the 10-inch tube pan is most popular. Angel Loaf Cake provides another means of diversity—shape.

Angel Loaf Cake

Sift ½ cup sifted cake flour with ¼ cup sugar 2 times; set aside. Beat ¾ cup (6) egg whites with 1 teaspoon vanilla, ½ teaspoon cream of tartar, ¼ teaspoon almond extract, and dash salt till stiff enough to form soft peaks but still moist and glossy. Add ½ cup sugar, 2 tablespoons at a time, continuing to beat till egg whites hold stiff peaks.

Sift about a *third* of the flour mixture over whites; fold in. Repeat, folding in remaining flour in 2 additions. Bake in *ungreased* 9x5x3-inch loaf pan at 375° for 25 minutes or until done. Invert cake in pan; cool thoroughly.

Why angel food cakes fail

Angel cakes, delicate in flavor and texture, are achieved with accurately measured ingredients, proper preparation techniques, and carefully followed recipe directions. If a problem arises in the finished product, one of the following may be at fault:

Tough cake
Sugar proportion too low; overmixing; oven too hot

Coarse texture
Underbeaten egg whites; insufficient blending of ingredients; oven too low

Cracks in crust
Overbeaten egg whites; sugar proportion too high; oven too hot

Sticky crust
Sugar proportion too high; underbaked

Undersized cake
Underbeaten or overbeaten egg whites; overmixing; pan too large; oven too hot; cake removed from pan before cool

---

Angel cake variations can be as easy or as complex as desired. In Lemonade Angel Dessert the baked cake becomes an ingredient for a lavish refrigerator dessert. When used in this context, often it is most convenient to purchase the baked cake or to prepare one from a cake mix.

Lemonade Angel Dessert

Light and refreshing after a heavy meal—

   1 cup evaporated milk
         •   •   •
   1 11-ounce angel food cake
   1 envelope (1 tablespoon)
       unflavored gelatin
 ½ cup sugar
      Dash salt
   1 cup water
   2 beaten eggs
         •   •   •
   1 6-ounce can frozen lemonade
       concentrate
      Few drops yellow food coloring

Pour evaporated milk into freezer tray. Freeze till soft ice crystals form around edges. Meanwhile, rub brown crumbs from angel cake; cut cake into bite-size pieces (10 cups).

In medium saucepan combine gelatin, sugar, and salt; add water and eggs. Cook and stir over medium-low heat till gelatin dissolves and mixture thickens slightly; remove from heat. Stir in frozen concentrate and food coloring; chill till partially set.

In large mixer bowl whip chilled evaporated milk till soft peaks form. Fold in partially-set gelatin mixture. Gently fold in cake cubes. Turn into 9-inch springform pan. Chill till firm. Makes 10 to 12 servings.

How to serve: Normally angel food cake, because of its lightness, is served with little or no frosting. If a frosting is desired, thin confectioners' icing or sweetened whipped cream with light flavoring suits the delicate cake quality. Fresh fruit and fruit sauces are frequently served as accompaniments as are ice cream and other frozen desserts. Angel cake is most easily cut with a cake cutter or wet sharp knife.

Angel food cake mix: Here's a time- and trouble-saving shortcut to an inviting angel food cake. Specially prepared ingredients plus simple directions for blending the batter and baking the cake make for successful results. As with any mix, exact measure of essential additional ingredients is important. The creative cookery urge can be satisfied by adding small quantities of extra flavor ingredients or using desired fillings, toppings, or sauces.

Two basic types of angel food cake mix are on the market. Each requires only water as an additional ingredient. One type involves a two-step preparation of the batter; the other needs only a one-step blending operation. Both types yield acceptable cakes, adaptable to interesting dessert variations like Cherry Angel Roll. (See *Cake, Egg* for additional information.)

Cherry Angel Roll

There's a cake left to freeze for later use—

    1 package angel cake mix
        (2-step type)
        Sifted confectioners' sugar
            • • •
    1 20-ounce can tart red cherries
    ¾ cup granulated sugar
    3 tablespoons cornstarch
    2 tablespoons butter or margarine
    ¼ teaspoon red food coloring
    6 drops almond extract
        Sweetened whipped cream

Prepare angel cake mix following package directions. Turn *half* the batter into *greased* and floured 15½x10½x1-inch baking pan, spreading evenly.* Bake at 375° for 12 minutes. Loosen sides; turn out on towel sprinkled with sifted confectioners' sugar. While still hot roll cake and towel together, starting at narrow end of cake. Let cool on rack.

Meanwhile, drain cherries, reserving ¾ cup juice; set aside a few whole cherries for garnish. In small bowl combine sugar, cornstarch, and dash salt. Heat reserved cherry juice in saucepan to boiling; gradually stir into sugar mixture. Return to saucepan. Cook and stir till thick and bubbly. Stir in butter, food coloring, and extract; add cherries. Cool.

Unroll cake and spread with filling. Roll up. Place seam side down on serving tray. Trim with sweetened whipped cream and reserved cherries. Makes 10 to 12 servings.

*Remaining half of cake batter may be baked in *ungreased* 9x5x3-inch loaf pan at 375° for 30 minutes or till done.

Chocolate Ripple Cake

Turns into a mocha dessert when served with coffee ice cream—

    1 package angel cake mix
    1 3½-ounce can (1⅓ cups)
        flaked coconut
    ⅓ cup instant cocoa powder

Prepare angel cake mix following package directions. Combine coconut and cocoa. Place a *third* of the cake batter in *ungreased* 10-inch tube pan; top with *half* the coconut mixture. Repeat and top with remaining cake batter. Bake according to package directions.

ANGELICA *(an jel' uh kuh)*—1. A sweet, aromatic herb used as a flavoring agent. 2. The name for a sweet, fortified dessert wine or liqueur.

No magic other than the intriguing taste and aroma is attributed to angelica in modern times. Centuries ago it was considered a powerful charm to chase away evil spirits. The roots were also sought for various medicinal purposes.

Wild angelica grows in northern Europe and in some European mountain regions. All parts of this plant are processed for culinary uses, but most familiar in this country are the candied angelica stems used to flavor liqueurs and to decorate wedding cakes, fruitcakes, and cookies. The big hollow stalks that resemble pale green rhubarb are candied for this use.

Tea is brewed from both fresh and dried angelica leaves. Chopped leaves and stems make a flavorful garnish for delicate white fish, fruit salads, or fruit cups.

In the Lapland area, dried angelica roots are ground into flour to make a certain native bread. The dried seeds are also used as a flavoring. (See also *Herb.*)

ANGEL PIE—A dainty dessert made with crisp, tender meringue shell and creamy filling. A whipped cream topping and fruit garnish are often added. Angel pie is usually made in an 8- or 9-inch size.

Numerous fillings are possible for the meringue shell. Cream fillings such as lemon, orange, and strawberry are commonly used. Fold fruit into a cream filling or just use sweetened fresh fruit in the meringue shell. Ice cream balls may be piled into the shell and topped with chocolate, butterscotch, or fruit sauce.

An outstanding feature of the angel pie is the method of preparation. The shell and filling are made the night before or several hours before serving time. The need for last minute preparation is eliminated, so the hostess can be unhurried and fresh to enjoy her guests. Show off this attractive dessert and save time, too, by slicing and serving it at the table.

Meringue Shell

    3 egg whites
    1 teaspoon vanilla
    ¼ teaspoon cream of tartar
    Dash salt
    1 cup sugar

Have egg whites at room temperature. Add vanilla, cream of tartar, and salt. Beat till soft peaks form. *Gradually* add sugar, beating till very stiff peaks form and sugar is dissolved. (Meringue will be glossy.)

Cover baking sheet with plain ungreased brown paper. Using 9-inch round cake pan as a guide draw circle on paper. Spread meringue over drawn circle. Shape into shell with back of large spoon, making bottom ½ inch thick and sides about 1¾ inches high.

Bake at 275° for 1 hour. Turn off heat and let dry in oven (door closed) at least 2 hours. Makes one 9-inch meringue shell.

Party or summertime dessert

←Use either fresh or frozen strawberries in this delicate Strawberry Angel Pie. No one will suspect how easy it was to make.

Strawberry Angel Pie

    1 3-ounce package strawberry-flavored gelatin
    1 cup sliced fresh strawberries *or* 1 10-ounce package frozen sliced strawberries, thawed and drained
    1 cup whipping cream
    1 recipe Meringue Shell

Dissolve gelatin in 1¼ cups boiling water. Chill until gelatin mixture is partially set. Whip cream till soft peaks form; fold cream and strawberries into gelatin mixture. Chill until mixture mounds slightly when spooned.

Pile into Meringue Shell. Chill 4 to 6 hours or overnight. Top with additional whipped cream and berries, if desired. Serves 8.

In order to save time but still have an elegant dessert, the angel pie filling can be made from a pudding mix, pudding and pie filling mix, canned fruit, or frozen fruit. Top with frozen whipped dessert topping and fruit garnish. (See *Dessert, Meringue* for additional information.)

Mandarin Angel Pie

    1 3½-ounce package *regular* lemon pudding and pie filling mix
    ½ cup sugar
    3 egg yolks
    1 11-ounce can mandarin oranges
    1 tablespoon lemon juice
    ½ cup whipping cream
    1 recipe Meringue Shell

Combine pudding and pie filling mix, sugar, and ¼ cup water in saucepan. Blend in egg yolks. Drain mandarin oranges, reserving syrup. To syrup add lemon juice and enough water to make 1¾ cups. Stir into pudding mixture; cook and stir over medium heat till thick and bubbly. Remove from heat; cool.

Whip cream till soft peaks form. Fold cream and ¾ *cup* of the oranges into pudding mixture. Spoon into prepared Meringue Shell. Chill overnight. Top with remaining orange segments and, if desired, additional whipped cream. Makes 8 servings.

ANGELS ON HORSEBACK—Hot hors d'oeuvres of bacon-wrapped raw oysters baked until the bacon crisps, then served piping hot on buttered toast, often with lemon wedges or hollandaise sauce. In England they are popular as a savory at the end of the meal. In this country they are used as a cocktail accompaniment.

Angels on Horseback

        8 slices bacon
       16 shucked oysters
        4 slices bread, toasted
                • • •
            Leaf lettuce

Cut each slice of bacon in half, then wrap a half strip of bacon around each oyster. Fry in deep hot fat (375°) for about 3 minutes. Drain well on paper toweling.

Cut each toast slice into fourths; arrange on a leaf of lettuce. Put one bacon-wrapped oyster on each piece of toast. Serve hot as an appetizer. Makes 4 servings.

ANGLAISE, Á L' *(äñg glāz', äñg glez')*—A French term describing foods prepared in the English style. This style usually refers to boiled or poached foods.

ANGLAISE CUSTARD—Custard made of egg yolks, sugar, milk or cream, and various flavorings. This term is applied to two types of custard. Creme Anglaise or English Cream is a soft custard to be served warm or cool as a dessert sauce. A delicate molded custard, usually cooked by poaching and served with fruit, bears the same name. (See also *Custard.*)

ANISE *(an' is)*—A licorice-flavored herb belonging to the parsley family. The anise plant with its feathery leaves and tiny grayish-brown fruits (seeds) grows to a height of about two feet.

Anise is one of the first herbs to be mentioned in history. Early Greek, Roman, and Egyptian writings also refer to it because anise was valued for its reputed medicinal properties. As late as colonial America, local laws required every man to cultivate anise. The *Holy Bible* mentions anise as a tithing herb. The Romans, among others, used anise in food. Merchants in England in the 14th century paid a heavy tax when importing this seasoning herb.

The licoricelike flavored leaves and seeds of anise are usually dried for use. Today, aniseed is found both whole and ground on the supermarket spice shelf.

Glazed Anise Loaf

        1 package active dry yeast
          Sifted all-purpose flour
            (about 3 cups)
        2 to 3 teaspoons aniseed
                • • •
        ½ cup milk
        ⅓ cup butter or margarine
        ⅓ cup sugar
        ½ teaspoon salt
        1 slightly beaten egg
        1 teaspoon shredded lemon peel
        2 tablespoons lemon juice
                • • •
        Confectioners' Frosting

In large mixer bowl combine yeast, 1¼ cups flour, and aniseed. Heat milk, butter, sugar, and salt in saucepan just till warm, stirring occasionally to melt butter.

Add heated liquid to flour mixture in mixing bowl; add egg and lemon peel and juice. Beat at low speed on electric mixer ½ minute, scraping sides of bowl constantly. Beat 3 minutes at high speed. By hand stir in enough remaining flour to make soft dough.

On lightly floured surface knead dough until smooth and elastic (8 to 10 minutes). Place dough in lightly greased bowl, turning once to grease surface. Cover; let rise in warm place till double (1½ to 2 hours). Punch down; let rest 10 minutes. Shape into loaf. Place in a greased 8½x4½x2½-inch loaf pan. Cover; let rise till double (about 45 minutes).

Bake at 375° for 35 to 40 minutes or until done. (Place aluminum foil over top last 20 minutes.) Remove from pan; cool on rack.

Frost with *Confectioners' Frosting:* To ¾ cup sifted confectioners' sugar, add about 1 tablespoon light cream, ¼ teaspoon vanilla, and dash salt; stir till smooth.

Anise oil is distilled from aniseed. (Previously commercial oil came from the star-anise of China which is so named because its fruit spreads out like a star.) Small quantities of anise oil can usually be purchased from a drugstore.

Anise is among the most popular flavoring herbs in Europe. The anise flavor is traditionally associated with special Christmas cookies such as Springerle and with some European yeast breads. The licorice-like flavor of the aniseed makes it very popular in the cakes, cookies, sweet breads, and rolls of Italy, Greece, and particularly the Scandinavian countries.

How to use: Suggestions for using aniseed in home cooking include in or on appetizers, seafood-cocktail sauces, pot roasts, stews, baked pork chops, Chinese meat-vegetable combinations, cream sauces, cookies, sweet breads, fruit pies, sweet pickles, tea, and applesauce.

To crush the whole anise seeds for use in cooking, place them between sheets of waxed paper and roll with a rolling pin. This releases the seeds' full flavor.

Both fresh and dried anise leaves, crushed, can be used in home cooking to give an interesting flavor to some kinds of shellfish, meats, soups, stews, and sauces.

Taste buds come alive when man-sized portions of Glazed Anise Loaf are served. This licoricelike flavored yeast bread makes a delightfully different addition to a brunch menu.

Fresh anise leaves are a taste stimulant when they garnish fruit salads or cooked vegetables such as carrots and beets.

The oil is used commercially in the manufacture of candies, pastries, breads, licorice-flavored products, and liqueurs such as absinthe, anisette, and pernod. Use anise oil with care due to its high degree of concentration. (See *Flavoring, Herb* for additional information.)

Anise-Flavored Butter

Soften 1 teaspoon aniseed in 1 teaspoon boiling water for 30 minutes. Add to ½ cup softened butter; cream until fluffy. Serve with corn-on-the-cob or other cooked vegetables.

Dark Herb Cookies

    ½ cup shortening
    ½ cup sugar
    1 egg
    ½ cup molasses
    2¼ cups sifted all-purpose
          flour
    2 teaspoons baking soda
    3 teaspoons ground ginger
    1 teaspoon ground cinnamon
    ½ teaspoon ground cloves
    ¼ teaspoon salt
    ⅓ cup hot strong coffee
    2 tablespoons aniseed
    2 teaspoons coriander seed,
          crushed
          •   •   •
       Vanilla Glaze

Cream together shortening and sugar. Beat in egg; stir in molasses. Sift together flour, soda, ginger, cinnamon, cloves, and salt. Add dry ingredients to creamed mixture alternately with coffee, mixing thoroughly after each addition. Stir in aniseed and coriander seed.

Drop from teaspoon 2 inches apart on greased cookie sheet. Bake at 350° for 8 to 10 minutes. Remove from pan and cool on rack.

Frost with *Vanilla Glaze:* Combine 2 cups sifted confectioners' sugar, 1 teaspoon vanilla, and enough milk to make spreading consistency. Top each cookie with a walnut half. Makes about 3½ dozen cookies.

Jewel Candies

A delicate anise flavor perks up these candies. Color them red and green for Christmas—

       Butter or margarine
    1 cup sugar
    ½ cup light corn syrup
    ¼ teaspoon anise oil
       Food coloring

Line 8x8x2-inch pan with foil, extending foil up sides; butter foil. Butter sides of heavy 1-quart saucepan. In it combine sugar, syrup, and ⅓ cup water. Bring to boiling, stirring constantly till sugar is dissolved. Cook over medium heat to hard-crack stage (300°). Remove from heat; add anise oil and desired coloring. Immediately pour into prepared pan.

When the candy is just beginning to set around the edges, carefully lift foil out of pan (candy will still be runny and hot in center). With scissors, cut candy into 1-inch strips, beginning with outside edges. Then quickly, while candy is still pliable, cut into very small pieces of irregular shape. To work fast enough, this requires 2 or 3 people to cut. Make only one batch at a time. Makes ½ pound.

ANJOU PEAR *(an' jōō)*—A heart-shaped winter pear, medium to large in size, with a thin yellowish green skin sometimes tinged with red when ripe.

Anjou is the Americanized name of the French term *Beurre d'Anjou.* This succulent, winy-tasting pear originated in Belgium in 1819 where it was cultivated by Belgian and French monks. In 1842, Colonel Wilder of Boston, brought the Anjou pear to the United States.

The smooth texture, juiciness, and rich spicy flavor of this pear make it a favorite for fresh eating and salads. Anjou pears may also be broiled, baked with spices, or canned. (See also *Pear.*)

ANNATTO *(uh nat' ō)*—A tree of Central and South America and the Caribbean Islands that yields a seed of the same name. When crushed or steeped in vegetable oil, the seed yields a yellow red or orange red dye.

South American Indians use annatto for painting their bodies. Among the civilized communities it is principally used for coloring butter, cheese, and some Spanish-American foods. The seeds are used only for color as they have little flavor. Annatto is also known in Spanish America as achiote and in the Pacific area as achuete.

ANTIPASTO *(an′ ti pä′ stō)*—An Italian word for "before the pasta" that has become well known as meaning a type of appetizer or hot or cold hors d'oeuvre. In the United States the word antipasto is commonly used to refer to any assortment of Italian appetizers.

A variety of savory foods, mixed in oil or vinegar and seasoned with spices or herbs, makes up an antipasto service. Attractively arranged flat glass jars of antipasto foods are widely marketed. The name "antipasto" is also given to foods, such as Antipasto Sandwich, which are filled with a variety of Italian-style foods.

Antipasto can be as simple as slices of ham rolled around melon balls, or as elaborate as dozens of foods displayed in small dishes. Many fine restaurants provide the latter-type antipasto for guests to enjoy. At home serve antipasto in an attractive arrangement either on one big serving platter or on individual serving plates.

Antipasto foods are usually fork- rather than finger-foods so be sure to supply guests with individual plates and forks when they are served.

Antipasto Sandwich

Cut a round loaf of bread crosswise into four slices. Before filling each layer, sprinkle the bread with wine vinegar, olive *or* salad oil, and dried oregano leaves, crushed. Place bologna slices, green pepper wedges, canned pimiento strips, and chicory leaves on the bottom slice of bread for first layer.

Top with second slice of bread. Layer with shredded lettuce, sliced tomatoes, hard-cooked egg slices, and anchovies.

Top with third piece of bread. Layer with hard salami, provolone cheese, and thin onion slices. Top with remaining bread slice. Skewer sandwich with long bamboo skewers to hold together. Garnish with parsley fluffs, if desired. Cut in wedges. Makes 4 servings.

Individual Antipasto

Prepare pepper cups to hold individual servings by slicing off tops of fresh green peppers and scooping out the seeds and membrane. If necessary, cut thin slice off bottom to make them sit flat. Stuff with Marinated Artichoke Hearts, stuffed green and ripe olives, pickles, tomato wedges, and hot peppers.

Add green onions, celery, and carrot sticks. Serve with cornucopias of salami slices twisted around cheese sticks.

Marinated Artichoke Hearts

   1 **9-ounce package frozen artichoke hearts** *or* **1 16-ounce can artichoke hearts**

        • • •

   3 **tablespoons olive** *or* **salad oil**
2½ **tablespoons lemon juice**
   1 **envelope Italian salad dressing mix**

Cook frozen artichoke hearts according to package directions (*or* drain and halve canned artichokes). Combine olive *or* salad oil, lemon juice, and salad dressing mix in screw-top jar; shake to mix. Pour over artichokes. Chill thoroughly, basting with marinade a few times. Drain well before using.

Individual Antipasto features a relish assortment including Marinated Artichoke Hearts in crisp green pepper cups.

Antipasto

Arrange some or all of the following on serving plates: chilled tuna in lettuce cups, cheese wedges, pepperoni slices, olives, radish roses, pickled peppers, honeydew balls wrapped with prosciutto ham, cherry tomatoes, marinated artichoke hearts.

Antipasto is one of several foods served as an appetizer and should be served in an attractive arrangement that enhances the foods being used. (See also *Appetizer*.)

APERITIF *(ä per′ i tēf′)*—A French word designating an alcoholic beverage served as an appetite stimulant before a meal. The qualities which make a drink a good aperitif are cleanness of taste, coldness, dryness, and tartness or bitterness.

In Europe, an aperitif is usually a wine or a wine-based drink. Other countries, however, have broadened the term to include all types of alcoholic beverages served before a meal.

Although aperitif wines have long been served in Europe, the custom was not adopted in the United States until this century. In earlier centuries, social drinking took place after the meal. During the past century, however, the cocktail hour has become a custom before dinner. Aperitifs such as wine or a cocktail are served during this social hour to put the diners in the right frame of mind for eating.

Europeans usually drink wine-based aperitifs without chilling them but many Americans prefer to chill all types of aperitifs. Since ice dilutes the wine, it should be chilled in the refrigerator.

Absinthe, a green liqueur with an aromatic anise flavor, is probably the most historically famous aperitif. However, because it is highly toxic, absinthe is now banned in most countries. Popular substitutes for absinthe include Pernod and Ricard. These aperitifs are customarily mixed with water and served with ice.

American wineries now produce 50 or more different aperitif wines, many with exotic names and flavored with natural food flavors. Flavored wines are served chilled or over ice with sparkling water.

Among the popular aperitif wines are dry sherry, dry or sweet vermouth, any dry white wine, champagne, and the other sparkling wines.

Some aperitifs contain various mixtures of herbs that give distinctively bitter flavors. These are generally served straight (undiluted) or on ice. If a bit of sweetening is desired, a touch of grenadine syrup or simple syrup can be added.

The use of the aperitif as an appetizer has led to the somewhat colloquial use of the name for nonalcoholic liquids served before a meal. Using the term this way, fruit juice or a vegetable juice cocktail is sometimes referred to as an aperitif. (See also *Wines and Spirits*.)

APOLLINARIS WATER *(ä pŏl′ ĭ när′ ĭs)*—A highly aerated alkaline mineral water from a spring in Germany used as a table water because it has no taste.

APPETITE—An instinctive desire or tendency to satisfy with food the needs or cravings of the body. Hunger is the sensation of a real need for food. Appetite, on the other hand, is the anticipation of pleasure to be gained from eating or drinking. Phychologists classify appetite as a compound emotion consisting of two parts —desire and satisfaction. This emotion is not limited to food but can also be expressed toward money and possessions.

Appetite may rise "by the clock" in persons who have very regular eating habits. It is stimulated by the sight, aroma, and appearance of food, real or imagined, and may spring up just from thinking about food. It's a boon to the cook who likes to have her family and guests come to the table with appetites aroused to enjoy the meal she has prepared.

Appetite may also disappear suddenly without being gratified or after the consumption of a few mouthfuls.

Serve an antipasto meal

This Antipasto doubles as a meal for one→ or an appetizer for several. Meats, vegetables, and fruits all appear here.

APPETIZER

Ingenious ideas for planning and serving these important foods simply but elegantly.

Appetizer, a derivation of the word appetite, is a small portion of food or drink served ahead of the meal to stimulate the appetite. Each should be a delight to the eye as well as to the palate. Likewise, artful, even peppy, appetizers create a desire for more food.

Rarely served in America before 1900, appetizers have skyrocketed in popularity since the turn of the century. Today when guests are expected, American hostesses comb cook books and magazines in planning an appetizer course. Fortunately, appetizers are not limited to party time, though, for they have become an established part of family mealtime too.

The foods served for party appetizers have gained such fame that many a menu for a holiday open house, buffet, reception, or cocktail party consists exclusively of spectacular appetizers and punch, coffee, or other beverages.

First courses similar to the American appetizer are widely known around the world. The French, Slavs, Scandinavians, and Italians each have their traditional dishes with which to tempt the appetite.

From France come the hors d'oeuvres, the small pieces of cheese, meat, fish, or olives often served with a flourish on a silver tray. The name hors d'oeuvres carries over when these same foods are put together in more elaborate combinations to be eaten with a fork.

Zakouska, a meal-before-a-meal, is eaten in Russia and other Slavic countries. Small, savory pieces of food similar to the hors d'oeuvre are accompanied by generous amounts of wine and liquor. Formerly the zakouska was reserved for an antechamber or a room outside the dining room. Now it may be arranged on trays and served at the main dining room table.

In Scandinavian countries the prelude to the main course is the smorgasbord, which means "the bread and butter table." This is a buffet table which boasts dozens of delicacies both hot and cold. Decisions are difficult when selecting from smoked and pickled herring, several cheeses, salads, and meats. Smorgasbord from a bountiful table can also be the entrée.

The Italian first course is antipasto, a robust assortment of tangy, savory foods. Here olives, anchovies, sliced sausages, artichoke hearts, cheeses, and fish are important foods served ahead of the meal.

Varieties of appetizers

Appetizers in America include an array of foods. The first course might be a cocktail, fondue, canapé, hors d'oeuvres, dip, spread, tidbit, relish or juice.

A cocktail is usually made of seafood, fruits, or vegetables accompanied by a sauce or dressing. One of the better known examples is shrimp served with a highly-seasoned sauce made from a chili sauce base; this is the popular shrimp cocktail.

Crab Cocktail

Flake 1 cup freshly cooked *or* one 7½-ounce can crab meat, removing cartilage. Mix with 1 cup finely chopped celery; chill. Serve in lettuce-lined cocktail cups with a cocktail sauce.

Begin with a fondue

Spear Teriyaki Meatballs on long bamboo → skewers and let everyone join in the fun of cooking in a bubbling fondue pot.

Fondue involves the guest in the actual preparation of the appetizer. Tiny pieces of meat speared on long forks are cooked in hot oil, or bits of bread are swirled in a cheese mixture. Usually the guests sit around a table, but the fondue can be dipped while standing.

Teriyaki Meatballs

      1 tablespoon soy sauce
      1 tablespoon water
      2 teaspoons sugar
    1/4 teaspoon instant minced onion
        Dash garlic salt
        Dash monosodium glutamate
        Dash ground ginger
    1/2 pound ground round
    1/2 cup fine soft bread crumbs
        Salad oil

Combine soy sauce, water, sugar, onion, garlic salt, monosodium glutamate, and ginger; let stand 10 minutes. Combine ground round and bread crumbs; stir in soy sauce mixture.

Shape into 3/4-inch balls. Spear meatballs on bamboo skewers; cook in deep hot fat (375°) in a fondue pot about 1 1/2 minutes. Serve with catsup, mustard, and mayonnaise mixed with dill pickles. Makes about 2 1/2 dozen balls.

Both canapés and hors d'oeuvres are defined as small, savory servings of food. Canapés are made on a bread, cracker, or pastry base and may be eaten with the fingers. Hors d'oeuvres, unlike canapés, are not made on a base and should be eaten with a knife and fork. Either food can be served hot or cold.

Asparagus Fold-Overs

Trim crusts from slices of sandwich bread; roll flat. Prepare one envelope hollandaise sauce mix according to directions; spread on bread. Sprinkle with Parmesan cheese and place one canned asparagus spear diagonally on each. Fold opposite corners over spear and secure with wooden pick. Brush with butter or margarine; sprinkle with Parmesan cheese. Bake at 400° for 12 minutes or till bread is browned.

Stuffed Mushrooms

Serve these hors d'oeuvres sizzling hot—

      2 6-ounce cans broiled mushroom
        crowns*
      1 tablespoon finely chopped onion
      1 teaspoon salad oil
    1/4 cup finely chopped salami
    1/4 cup smoke-flavored cheese
        spread
      1 tablespoon catsup
        Fine soft bread crumbs

Drain mushrooms. Hollow out crowns and chop enough pieces to make 3 tablespoons; cook pieces with onion in oil. Stir in salami, cheese spread, and catsup. Stuff into mushroom crowns; sprinkle with crumbs. Bake on baking sheet at 425° for 6 to 8 minutes.

*Or use 2 pints fresh mushrooms. Wash; trim off tips of stems. Remove stems and chop enough pieces to make 1/3 cup. Continue recipe as above.

A juice appetizer is served hot, cold, or at room temperature. One juice or a combination of juices, flavors, and seasonings can be included in the drink. Alcoholic beverages may or may not be mixed with the juice.

Spiced Cranberry Drink

      6 whole cloves
      6 inches stick cinnamon
      4 whole cardamom, shelled
            • • •
      4 cups cranberry juice cocktail
      1 cup light raisins
    1/4 cup sugar
      2 cups port wine

Tie spices in cheesecloth bag; place in saucepan. Add *2 cups* of cranberry cocktail, raisins, and sugar; bring to boiling. Simmer uncovered for 10 minutes. Remove spice bag.

Before serving, add remaining cranberry cocktail and wine. Heat almost to boiling. Pour into heat-proof serving pitcher or bowl. Serve in mugs or punch cups, adding a few of the raisins to each. Makes about 6 cups.

Well-seasoned pâté is sure to be a hit with hungry guests. Garnish Chicken Liver Pâté with lemon wedges and chopped egg. Serve with assorted crackers, relishes, and tomato juice.

Spreads are rather firm mixtures shaped into balls, logs, or rolls. Guests serve themselves by spreading the mixture with a knife or spoon onto bread, toast, or crackers. Pâté, made with ground meat and served cold, is a world-famous spread.

Chicken Liver Pâté

      Butter or margarine
  1 pound chicken livers
  3 tablespoons mayonnaise or
      salad dressing
  2 tablespoons lemon juice
  2 tablespoons butter or margarine,
      softened
  1 tablespoon minced onion
  8 to 10 drops bottled hot pepper
      sauce
  ½ teaspoon dry mustard
  ½ teaspoon salt
      Dash pepper

In saucepan melt small amount of butter. Add livers; cook covered, stirring occasionally, till livers are no longer pink. Put livers through food mill; blend with mayonnaise, lemon juice, the 2 tablespoons butter, onion, hot pepper sauce, mustard, salt, and pepper.

Shape mixture in 2½-cup mold. Chill several hours; carefully unmold. Garnish with chopped hard-cooked egg, if desired.

Relishes, an assortment of cold, crisp vegetables, pickles, olives, pickled vegetables, or pickled fruits, are usually arranged on platters or trays which are passed among the guests.

Tidbits are the simplest form of appetizer. Small foods including nuts, olives, cheese cubes, potato chips, and cereal-nut mixtures are served in small bowls or on trays placed around the room. They may be eaten with the fingers, or speared with cocktail forks or wooden picks.

Serve dunkers that are as imaginative as the dips themselves. With mild-flavored dips such as Cheese Fluff use fruits in season. Seedless green grapes, strawberries, cherries, pears, and apple slices are bright and tasty. Dip fruit that might turn dark in orange juice or color keeper before serving. Stout-flavored Jiffy Braunschweiger Dip is excellent with crisp corn-chip, green-onion, radish-rose, cracker, cucumber-round, and carrot-stick dunkers.

Plump Prunes

Pour boiling water over prunes; let stand till water cools. Drain and remove pits. *Or* use pitted, "moisturized" prunes.

Stuff prunes with pineapple cheese spread, pimento spread, bacon-flavored cheese, or other cheese spread. Top each with crisp walnut half.

Dips which have become very popular with the American public are soft, creamy mixtures scooped up on crackers, chips, fruits, or vegetables. These must never be so thin that they drip. To provide smooth, neat service, avoid serving with large groups or children's groups.

Jiffy Braunschweiger Dip

> 1 8-ounce roll braunschweiger
> 1 cup dairy sour cream
> ½ 8-ounce package blue cheese salad dressing mix

Combine all ingredients and blend thoroughly. Chill; serve with assorted crackers and vegetable sticks for dipping.

Cheese Fluff

Beat softened cream cheese till fluffy. Blend in tangy fruit juice to desired consistency. Top with grated fruit peel. Serve with fruit.

Planning appetizers

The selection of appetizers is limited only by one's imagination. They can express the party mood, carry out a theme, or be designed solely to impress the guests with the hostess' culinary talents.

When deciding on appetizers, consider the complete menu, how much time will be needed to prepare them, and what equipment will be available to keep them hot or cold as necessary. Part of the trick of successful planning is to avoid duplicating foods that will be served at later courses. For example, if tomatoes are in the tossed salad, skip tomato juice as the menu starter. Variety intrigues the taste and makes the whole meal more exciting. The appetizer, too, should not compete with the main dish in seasoning. A highly seasoned food may be served for the appetizer, but it must not be so strong as to overpower the taste of the main dish or steal interest from the main course.

All the food and beverage served during the appetizer should be coordinated in flavor. For example, peppy cheese or sausage bites are delicious with tomato juice while delicate salmon or turkey canapés are pleasing with fruit punch. If the main course planned is to be fairly substantial, the appetizer should be light. Serve tidbits such as bowls of olives or nuts, plates of crisp cheese sticks or wafers, or assorted raw vegetables with coarse salt on the side for dipping. Likewise, sturdier appetizers can be served with a meal which is light.

One or two types of appetizers is enough to serve with any meal. Guest invariably will sample each type of appetizer that is presented. If the variety is too large, the appetizer course might be too filling. A good plan is to have four or five canapés or hors d'oeuvres per person. If dinner is to be served late, allow six or seven per person. This will keep the guest's hunger at bay until time for the next course.

Consider the likes and dislikes of the guests. Introduce a new food to the group but avoid one which has unpleasant associations or very limited popularity. If some of the guests have dietary or religious restrictions, include a selection which they can eat and enjoy.

Plan to use foods which are in season. This will set a theme for the dinner. For instance, serve fresh fruits in the summer and nuts in the fall. These foods will be more plentiful and more economical. A complete reverse is quite intriguing. Serve cantaloupe and watermelon balls in the winter. Plan ahead and freeze fresh fruits during the summer when they have become monotonous. A few months later they will be a rare treat.

Appetizers may be either fancy or simple. Fancy appetizers require more time, various equipment to prepare, and adequate storage. Especially during holidays and special occasions, many hostesses enjoy going all-out and using their creative talents in preparing the appetizers. When planned to carry out the holiday theme, these appetizers can double as decorations.

Simple appetizers can be imaginatively served and require very little time and effort. A bowlful of creamy cottage cheese dip surrounded by cherry tomatoes is colorful and delicious. Use a mug or small pitcher to hold the carrot sticks and celery stalks passed as dippers.

Consider the equipment available. Are the utensils and containers that will be needed to prepare and store the food easily accessible? Often these items can be improvised, borrowed, or rented.

Refrigerator and freezer space, too, should be taken into consideration. Avoid individual servings of a cocktail that must be refrigerated, for instance, if the refrigerator will be needed to store salads, drinks, or desserts. The same holds true for the oven space. Hot appetizers would be difficult to prepare if the oven is needed for the main dish and rolls, or if different temperatures are required.

Consider, also, how the appetizer will be served. Hot appetizers should be served piping hot, and cold appetizers should be served thoroughly chilled. Attractive appliances and equipment are on the market which will keep food warm or cold while being served. If the appetizer is to be served at the table, select foods that can be placed on the table and remain at room temperature for a time without losing their best flavor and appearance since it usually takes the guests a while to be seated.

Plan appetizers that can be served in the dishes which are available. If the necessary equipment is not obtainable, then it is best to select something else which can be served properly with the dishes on hand.

Serve appetizers that can be handled easily. Since the first course will set the mood for the entire meal, the hostess should prepare appetizers which she can serve in a relaxed manner. This might be an appetizer which is made in advance or with little effort just before serving.

When the appetizer course is served in the living room, cleanup could be a problem, especially if guests will return after the meal. The homemaker without extra help might ask one of the guests to assist. Or, by planning to use few dishes or colorful paperware, the hostess can manage the clearing away by herself.

Be prepared for the unexpected by keeping appetizer supplies on hand. Have a supply of bread in the freezer, canned fillings and dips, a variety of seasonings for butters, and garnishes in the refrigerator or freezer. Then you are ready for the unexpected guest or guest that eats more than anticipated.

How to serve: Appetizers should be served in a grand style to set the mood for the first course as well as the entire meal. The atmosphere in which the appetizers are served, where they are served, their appearance, and how they are served are the key elements in creating a style.

Appetizers are basically informal in nature. They start the meal in a pleasant mood—when served by a smiling, relaxed host and hostess. Guests feel welcomed and become acquainted easily with one another during the appetizer course.

The patio, living room, dining room, or wherever guests gather are appropriate locations for the appetizer course. Appetizers that are to be served in the living room or on the patio are usually arranged

Appetizer Cheese Mousse, a make-ahead appetizer or snack, is cool and zesty. Use crisp parsley and carrot curls for garnishing. Spread on crackers and serve with fruit, if desired.

on trays and platters which are passed among the guests, or on small dishes which are placed around the room. If space permits, a small appetizer buffet can be served. Finger foods such as relishes, tidbits, canapés, dips, and spreads can be accompanied by a cup or glass of beverage. Provide plates or napkins for the guests to put their food on as they sit or move about the room.

Appetizers that require a knife and fork or spoon should be served at the dining table. Hors d'oeuvres, cocktails, and foods which are difficult to eat with the fingers are examples. This course is usually placed on the table before the guests enter the dining room.

Attractively served appetizers are more tempting. Arrange food so it is easy to serve as well as having eye-appeal.

Group types of appetizers together. It will be easier for the guests to identify and decide which to take. Place individual pieces so that one piece can be taken without touching the others.

An attractive way to arrange a platter is to place an orange or grapefruit half in the center, cut side down. Insert wooden picks in the skin of the fruit. Place stuffed olives, tiny onions, cocktail sausages, cheese cubes, and assorted tidbits on the other ends of the picks. Arrange hors d'oeuvres and canapés around this centerpiece, or if desired, use this arrangement on a small platter by itself. A lime or lemon half in a small dish makes a handy, colorful holder for wooden picks when serving an appetizer that requires picks for self-service.

Ingenious serving bowls can be made from avocado shells, pineapple halves, green pepper, lobster shells, and Gouda or Edam cheese. Simply scoop out the food leaving a thin shell. Then pile a dip, spread, or fruit mixture into the cavity. This is a perfect container and a good way to supplement the supply of dishes.

Garnishes add the finishing touch to the appetizers. A garnish must always be edible. A lemon wedge, a twist of candied orange rind, or a scoop of sherbet to top off a fruit cup gives color and a professional touch. Frost the rims of glasses by dipping into lemon juice, then in confectioners' sugar. Chill the glasses for at least half an hour. Long cocktail or wooden picks studded with melon balls, strawberries, orange sections, or tangerine sections make swizzle sticks for juices. Frosted grapes, cherries, anchovy fillets, olives, pimiento strips, and nuts are also attractive garnish additions for appetizers.

The host or children in the family can assist the hostess in passing the appetizers so she will be free to attend to other duties. The food should be passed among the guests every five or ten minutes or as the guests are ready for refills. The trays are left in a centrally located area so the guests may help themselves between the passings.

A good plan is to have a duplicate platter arranged and left in the kitchen. When the original platter needs refilling, the hostess can bring out the second one with no effort or wasted time.

The serving dishes, glasses, and plates can be removed quickly if they are collected on the serving tray or on trays placed in the room for this purpose as the guests have finished with them.

Make-ahead appetizers

Appetizers which can be made ahead relieve the hostess of extra work at serving time. The food is prepared earlier in the day or several days ahead. Whether stored in the refrigerator, freezer, or airtight containers, extra care should be taken to see that the appetizers keep their best quality: bread should be soft, gelatin firm, crackers crisp.

The dishes and utensils used in preparation can be cleaned and put away long before the meal is to be served. Not only will the kitchen be neater, but there will be more space for any last minute preparations that are necessary for the other courses. When the supply of kitchen utensils is limited, pre-preparation of the appetizers will leave many utensils available for the last-minute meal preparations.

When serving made-ahead appetizers, the hostess is confident that the food is delicious, attractive, and most importantly, ready. This allows her a few minutes for final touches or relaxing before greeting her guests, assured that the first course will be a success.

Appetizer Cheese Mousse

2 teaspoons unflavored gelatin
¼ cup cold water
2 cups dairy sour cream
1 8-ounce carton (1 cup) small
  curd cream-style cottage
  cheese
¼ cup crumbled blue cheese
2 teaspoons Italian salad dressing
  mix

In small saucepan soften gelatin in cold water. Heat over low heat stirring till gelatin dissolves. Stir gelatin into sour cream; add cottage cheese, blue cheese, and salad dressing mix. Beat with electric or rotary beater till well blended. Pour into 3½-cup ring mold or small loaf pan. Chill till firm; unmold.

Salmon Party Log

Tangy salmon rolled in pecans and parsley—

1 16-ounce can (2 cups) salmon
1 8-ounce package cream cheese,
  softened
1 tablespoon lemon juice
2 teaspoons grated onion
1 teaspoon prepared horseradish
¼ teaspoon salt
¼ teaspoon liquid smoke
½ cup chopped pecans
3 tablespoons snipped parsley

Drain and flake salmon, removing skin and bones. Combine salmon, cream cheese, lemon juice, onion, horseradish, salt, and liquid smoke; mix thoroughly. Chill several hours. Combine pecans and parsley. Shape salmon mixture in 8x2-inch log; roll in nut mixture; chill well. Pass with crackers.

Edam Sage Spread

Makes its own serving dish—

1 whole Edam cheese, about 8
  ounces
1 cup dairy sour cream
1 teaspoon ground sage
  Dash onion powder

Have cheese at room temperature. Using a sawtooth cut, remove top of whole Edam cheese. Carefully scoop out cheese, leaving a thin shell. Finely chop cheese; mix with sour cream, sage, and onion powder.

Spoon cheese mixture into Edam shell; chill thoroughly. Arrange on tray with assorted crackers. Makes about 2 cups cheese spread.

Ham Ball

Frosted with cream cheese—

2 4½-ounce cans deviled ham
3 tablespoons chopped pimiento-
  stuffed green olives
1 tablespoon prepared mustard
  Bottled hot pepper sauce
        • • •
1 3-ounce package cream cheese,
  softened
2 teaspoons milk

Blend ham, olives, mustard, and pepper sauce to taste. Form in ball on serving dish; chill. Combine cream cheese and milk; frost ham ball. Chill; remove from refrigerator 15 minutes before serving. Garnish with parsley. Pass with assorted crackers.

Braunschweiger Glacé

1 envelope (1 tablespoon)
  unflavored gelatin
½ cup cold water
1 10½-ounce can condensed
  consommé
        • • •
½ pound (1 cup) braunschweiger
3 tablespoons mayonnaise or salad
  dressing
1 tablespoon vinegar
1 tablespoon minced onion

Soften gelatin in cold water and consommé. Heat to boiling, stirring to dissolve gelatin. Pour into 2½-cup mold; chill till firm.

Blend braunschweiger, mayonnaise, vinegar, and onion. Spoon out center of firm consommé, leaving ½-inch shell. Fill with meat mixture. Heat the spooned-out consommé till melted; pour over meat. Chill till firm. Unmold.

Smoky Ham and Cheese Spread

1 6-ounce package smoky cheese
   spread
1 3-ounce can deviled ham
¼ cup chopped dill pickle
1 teaspoon Dijon-style mustard
⅛ teaspoon salt
   Celery sticks, chilled

Combine all ingredients except celery; blend thoroughly. Chill ham mixture. Stuff ham mixture into celery and serve.

Ginger Dip

Accented with water chestnuts—

½ cup mayonnaise or salad
   dressing
½ cup dairy sour cream
2 tablespoons snipped parsley
2 tablespoons finely chopped
   canned water chestnuts
1 tablespoon finely chopped onion
1 tablespoon finely chopped
   candied ginger
1 clove garlic, minced
1½ teaspoons soy sauce

Combine mayonnaise and sour cream. Stir in parsley, chestnuts, onion, ginger, garlic, and soy sauce. Chill. Serve with sesame crackers or chips for dipping. Makes 1¼ cups.

Creamy Cottage Cheese Dip

Quick and easy to make—

1 12-ounce carton (1½ cups)
   cream-style cottage cheese
1 tablespoon mayonnaise or salad
   dressing
1 teaspoon salad-spice-and-herb
   mix
   Parsley

Combine cottage cheese, mayonnaise, and salad-spice-and-herb mix. Blend in blender or with electric mixer until almost smooth. Chill. Sprinkle with parsley. Serve with celery and carrot sticks. Makes 1½ cups.

Hot Sausage-Bean Dip

½ pound bulk pork sausage
1 16-ounce can pork and beans
   in tomato sauce
2 ounces sharp process American
   cheese, shredded (½ cup)
2 tablespoons catsup
½ teaspoon prepared mustard
   Few drops bottled hot pepper
   sauce

In skillet break sausage into small pieces. Cook slowly until browned, about 10 minutes. Drain off fat. In blender combine sausage, beans, shredded cheese, catsup, mustard, and hot pepper sauce; blend till smooth, stopping occasionally to scrape down sides.

Return to skillet and heat. Serve with corn chips. Makes 2½ cups.

Crisp, cheesy Welcome Wafers served with one or more fresh vegetables such as cherry tomatoes are sure to tempt the appetite.

Rainbow Mint Julep, a kaleidoscope of melon balls accented
with a blend of tangy fruit juices and sparkling carbonated
beverages, provides a sweet, cool appetizer for summertime.

Marinated Beef Strips

Hardy enough to please the men—

> 1 pound cooked sirloin steak
>   *or* beef roast, cut in thin
>   strips
> 1 small onion, thinly sliced and
>   separated in rings
> ¾ teaspoon salt
>   Dash pepper
> 1½ tablespoons lemon juice
> 1 cup dairy sour cream

Combine beef, onion rings, salt, and pepper.
Sprinkle with lemon juice. Stir in sour cream.
Chill. Serve on lettuce. Serves 6.

Welcome Wafers

Strongly flavored with garlic and blue cheese—

> ¾ cup butter or margarine,
>   softened
> ½ cup shredded Cheddar cheese
> ⅓ cup crumbled blue cheese
> 2 cups sifted all-purpose flour
> ½ clove garlic, minced
> 1 teaspoon snipped parsley
> 1 teaspoon snipped chives

Cream butter, cheddar cheese, and blue cheese.
Mix in flour, garlic, parsley, and chives. Shape
in 1½-inch rolls; chill. Slice and bake at 375°
for 8 to 10 minutes.

Rainbow Melon Julep

Make with sugar or non-caloric sweetener—

> 2 teaspoons shredded orange peel
> 2 teaspoons shredded lime peel
> ½ cup orange juice
> ½ cup lime juice
> 2 to 4 tablespoons sugar *or* non-
>   caloric liquid sweetener to
>   equal 2 to 4 tablespoons sugar
> 2 tablespoons chopped fresh mint
> 8 cups melon balls (watermelon,
>   cantaloupe, honeydew)
> 1 cup lemon-lime carbonated
>   beverage *or* low-calorie lemon-
>   lime carbonated beverage,
>   chilled
> Mint sprigs (optional)

Combine peels, juices, sugar, and mint; pour over melon balls. Chill at least 2 hours. Just before serving, pour carbonated beverage over fruit. Garnish with mint sprigs, if desired. Makes eight 1-cup servings.

Snappy Cheese Appetizers

Crisp and crunchy—and they're quick to make—

> 2 sticks piecrust mix
> 1 4-ounce package shredded sharp
>   natural Cheddar cheese (1 cup)
> 2 teaspoons paprika
> ¼ teaspoon dry mustard
>
> • • •
>
> 30 small pimiento-stuffed green
>   olives

Prepare piecrust mix according to package directions, thoroughly mixing in cheese, paprika, and mustard, till mixture forms a ball. Divide dough in half. Using *half* the dough wrap about one teaspoon around each olive.

Roll other half of dough on floured surface to 12x8-inch rectangle. With pastry wheel or knife cut into sticks ½ inch wide and 4 inches long. Place olive balls and cheese sticks on ungreased baking sheet. Bake at 425° for 10 to 12 minutes or till golden brown.

Serve as appetizers, snacks, or salad accompaniments. Makes 2½ dozen olive balls and 4 dozen cheese sticks.

All three of these appetizers are finger foods. Bull's-Eye Meatballs, top, are served sizzling hot from the broiler. Gala Fruit Skewers, middle, are low in calories and simple to make. Just spear an assortment of pineapple chunks, mandarin orange sections, banana slices, grapes, cherries, and melon balls on wooden picks. Plunge the paper decorated pick into a citrus fruit for serving. Smoky Ham and Cheese Spread, bottom, is great stuffed into crisp celery sticks.

Deviled Almonds

Snappy nuts for munching—

1½ cups blanched whole almonds
¼ cup butter or margarine
¼ cup salad oil

. . .

1 tablespoon celery salt
½ teaspoon salt
½ teaspoon chili powder
⅛ teaspoon cayenne

In heavy skillet combine almonds, butter, and salad oil. Cook and stir over medium heat till almonds are golden brown. Remove almonds and drain on paper toweling.

Combine celery salt, salt, chili powder, and cayenne. Sprinkle over hot almonds; stir to coat completely. Makes 1½ cups.

Last-minute appetizers

Many appetizers must be prepared just before serving. However, with careful planning and *advance* preparation, mouthwatering appetizers can be achieved with a minimum of effort and anxiety.

Use an appetizer recipe at least once before making it for guests; this is no time to be experimenting. A familiar recipe will be easier to prepare because you can anticipate how long each step will take and will know how the final product is supposed to look.

Before the actual preparation time, think through the recipe step-by-step. Actually rehearse the preparation of the appetizer to be sure all the steps are understood. Set out the equipment, utensils, and serving dishes that will be needed.

Double-check to be sure that all the ingredients are available in sufficient amounts. Pre-measure as much as possible: chop vegetables, measure dry ingredients and wrap in waxed paper; grate cheese and wrap in plastic wrap, and squeeze juices. Avoid measuring or opening ingredients which might lose their flavor as, for instance, extracts. Just before time to serve the appetizer, proceed with the recipe steps. The food will be prepared more quickly and with less worry because much of the work has been done.

Combine Spicy Beef Dip and Shrimp in Jackets with Edam Sage Spread and Spiced Cranberry Drink for a tasty quartet.

Proceed with any recipe steps which can be done in advance. Many ground meat mixtures, for example, can be mixed and shaped several hours ahead. Then at serving time, the final cooking is completed and they are ready to be served. Broiled grapefruit can be cut in halves, sections loosened, sprinkled with brown or white sugar, and dotted with butter in advance. Broil a few minutes before serving.

Appetizers which must be eaten hot will be easier to manage if cooked in stages so a portion will be ready to serve hot as the guests finish each batch.

Shrimp in Jackets

1 pound frozen medium, shelled
    shrimp, thawed
½ teaspoon garlic *or* onion salt
¾ pound bacon (about 15 slices),
    cut in thirds

Sprinkle shrimp with garlic *or* onion salt. Wrap each shrimp in ⅓ slice bacon. Arrange on broiler rack. Broil 3 or 4 inches from heat just till bacon is crisp and browned, 8 to 10 minutes; turn occasionally. Serve on wooden picks. Makes about 40.

Plum-Glazed Franks

¼ cup plum jelly
¼ cup finely chopped chutney
1 teaspoon vinegar
    Dash garlic salt
1 7-ounce package cocktail frank-
    furters *or* 1 4-ounce can
    Vienna sausages, halved

Mix jelly, chutney, vinegar, and garlic salt in small skillet or chafing dish. Add franks; heat through, stirring constantly. Serve hot with wooden picks for serving and eating.

Glazed Sausage Bites

Simmered in a Cantonese-flavored sauce—

1 pound bulk pork sausage
½ cup finely crushed saltine
    cracker crumbs
⅓ cup milk
1 slightly beaten egg
½ teaspoon dried sage leaves,
    crushed

• • •

½ cup water
¼ cup catsup
2 tablespoons brown sugar
1 tablespoon vinegar
1 tablespoon soy sauce

Combine sausage, cracker crumbs, milk, egg, and sage. Beat at high speed on electric mixer 5 minutes. Shape into 1¼-inch balls. (Mixture will be soft—wet hands to shape easily.)

In ungreased skillet brown meat slowly on all sides, about 10 minutes. Pour off excess fat. Combine water, catsup, brown sugar, vinegar, and soy sauce. Pour over meatballs. Cover and simmer 15 minutes, stirring occasionally. Makes 3 dozen sausage bites.

Fancy Franks

Lots of flavor appeal—

2 7-ounce packages cocktail
    frankfurters
1 13½-ounce can pineapple chunks,
    drained
½ cup chili sauce
½ cup currant jelly
1½ tablespoons lemon juice
1½ teaspoons prepared mustard

Combine all ingredients in skillet and simmer 15 minutes. Serve warm with wooden picks. (Half a lime on a small dish is a colorful holder for the picks.)

Cheese and Sausage Rolls

16 sausage links
16 slices bread
1 cup shredded process American
    cheese
¼ cup butter or margarine,
    softened

Cook and drain sausage links following package directions. Trim crusts from bread; roll flat. Mix cheese and butter together; spread on both sides of each bread slice. Roll a sausage in each slice. Bake on greased baking sheet at 400° for 10 to 12 minutes. Slice.

Party Potato Chips

Clever way to dress up potato chips—

Spread one 4-ounce package potato chips on cookie sheet and sprinkle with ½ cup shredded process American cheese. Sprinkle lightly with ground thyme, basil, or marjoram. Heat in 350° oven for 5 minutes, or till cheese melts. Serve while hot.

Hurry-up Ham Puffs

Pictures on left are step-by-step illustrations—

(Top picture) Slicing lengthwise, cut three ½-inch-thick slices from 1 loaf of unsliced bread. Toast the 3 slices on both sides. Combine two 4½-ounce cans deviled ham and 3 tablespoons finely chopped onion; spread on toast; bringing right to edges. Cut 15 pimiento-stuffed green olives *or* pitted ripe olives in half; arrange 10 halves on each toast slice.

(Middle picture) Beat 3 egg whites till stiff peaks form. Combine ½ cup mayonnaise or salad dressing, ½ teaspoon dry mustard, and dash salt; fold gently into beaten egg whites. Spoon a mound of mixture over each olive slice.

(Bottom picture) Bake at 400° till golden, about 10 to 12 minutes. Cut each slice into 10 pieces. Serve hot. Makes 30 appetizers.

Appetizer Pie

  1 hard-cooked egg, finely chopped
  1 tablespoon mayonnaise or salad
     dressing
    Dash dried dillweed
  1 4½-ounce can deviled ham
  1 teaspoon prepared horseradish
  1 teaspoon prepared mustard
  1 8-ounce package cream cheese,
     softened
  2 tablespoons crumbled blue
     cheese
  2 medium unpeeled cucumbers,
     scored
  1 6- or 7-inch unsliced round
     loaf rye bread
    Mayonnaise or salad dressing
  1 2-ounce jar caviar (optional)

Egg Filling: Combine eggs, mayonnaise, dillweed, and dash salt. *Ham Filling:* Combine ham, horseradish, and mustard. *Cheese Filling:* Beat cheeses till fluffy. Slice the cucumber thin; cut slices in half. Cut four ½-inch thick slices horizontally from center of rye loaf. Spread with mayonnaise or salad dressing.

For each pie: Spread Egg Filling in center of bread slice. Ring with Ham Filling, then Cheese Filling. Overlap cucumber atop cheese. Add band of caviar between cucumber and ham. Serve in wedges. Makes 4 pies.

Chicken Liver Boats

½ pound chicken livers
2 tablespoons all-purpose flour
2 tablespoons butter or margarine
2 tablespoons chopped onion
½ teaspoon steak sauce
¼ teaspoon salt
Dash pepper
¼ cup light cream
1 stick piecrust mix
Parmesan cheese
Paprika

Coat chicken livers with flour; cook with butter, onion, and steak sauce for 10 minutes. Add salt and pepper; mash well. Stir in cream.

Prepare piecrust mix according to package directions. Roll out; cut in 2¼-inch rounds. Place 1 teaspoon liver mixture on each pastry round. Pinch two opposite ends to form oval boats. Sprinkle with Parmesan cheese. Bake at 425° 10 minutes. Sprinkle with paprika.

Bull's-Eye Meatballs

10 slices white bread
Butter or margarine
1 pound ground beef
2 tablespoons grated onion
1 tablespoon Worcestershire sauce
1 teaspoon salt
Chili sauce

Cut four 1½-inch rounds from each bread slice; toast on one side and spread with butter or margarine on other side.

Combine ground beef, onion, Worcestershire sauce, and salt. Shape into 40 balls, making an indentation in each. Place on buttered bread rounds. Broil 4 inches from heat for 5 to 6 minutes or till meat is done. Fill centers with chili sauce. Serve hot.

Mexican Tostadas

Use fresh, frozen, or canned tortillas. (If tortillas are frozen, thaw.) Cut each tortilla in quarters. Fry in shallow hot fat about 4 minutes, turning once. Drain on paper toweling. Serve warm and salted, if desired. Serve with a favorite dip.

Hot Cheese Dip with Fruit

A variation on the fruit and cheese combination—

1 cup shredded sharp process American cheese
1 cup shredded process Swiss cheese
1 6-ounce can (⅔ cup) evaporated milk
1 tablespoon prepared mustard
1 teaspoon Worcestershire sauce
Dash bottled hot pepper sauce
¼ cup finely chopped canned pimiento
. . .
Apples or pears, cut in wedges

Place cheeses, milk, mustard, Worcestershire sauce, and hot pepper sauce in small saucepan or chafing dish. Cook over low heat, stirring until cheese melts and mixture is smooth. Remove from heat and stir in pimiento.

Serve hot from chafing dish for dipping with apple or pear wedges.

Spicy Beef Dip

Hot, meaty dip for a fall party—

1 pound ground beef
½ cup chopped onion
1 clove garlic, minced
1 8-ounce can (1 cup) tomato sauce
¼ cup catsup
1 teaspoon sugar
¾ teaspoon dried oregano leaves, crushed
1 8-ounce package cream cheese, softened
⅓ cup grated Parmesan cheese

Cook ground beef, onion, and garlic in skillet till meat is lightly browned and onion is tender. Stir in tomato sauce, catsup, sugar, and oregano. Cover; simmer gently for 10 minutes. Spoon off excess fat.

Remove from heat. Add cream cheese and Parmesan cheese. Heat and stir till cream cheese is melted and well blended. Keep warm in chafing dish or buffet server and serve with crackers. Makes 3 cups.

APPLE

Selected information on using one of nature's oldest and most widely grown fruits.

These edible fruits, usually juicy, round, and red or yellow, include more than 7,000 varieties; yet when or where the first apple tree grew is not definitely known. The biblical account of Adam and Eve does place apples in the Garden of Eden; but some historians believe another fruit was involved. Whether the true "forbidden fruit" or not, apples have influenced cultures and lives of many people.

Literature and art have alluded to apples over the centuries. Serpents and dragons guarded them; King Solomon and Arabians hailed apples as healing agents. To Greeks and Romans, they symbolized love and beauty, and Norsemen believed apples maintained the youth of their gods. In several sixteenth and seventeenth century paintings, moreover, apples are depicted as causing the downfall of man.

Controversy between historians continues as to whether the first apple tree grew in Asia or Europe. Prehistoric lake-dwelling remains in Switzerland show that apples were eaten and perhaps even preserved for the winter by drying them. Except in the far north, apple species flourished over Europe as much as 3,000 years ago.

Apples have been well-liked for so long that selective development and improvement of apple varieties also go back in history. For example, by 800 B.C. the Greeks had already written about certain budding and grafting methods necessary for apple tree reproduction.

A bushel and a peck

←Cider, Apple Butter, Spicy Baked Apples, and Homemade Mincemeat Pie (See *Mincemeat*) tempt the apple lover at harvesttime.

By the time America was discovered, apples had become an important fruit in Europe. When colonists migrated to North America, apple trees came, too. The first recorded planting was in 1629 by the Massachusetts Bay Colony. French settlers, in addition, scattered plants and seeds throughout the St. Lawrence River area.

The early American apples, because of their poor eating quality, were used primarily in the making of cider; but by 1725 they were as good for eating as for drinking. In the Pennsylvania-Dutch colonies, women soon learned expertly the technique of drying apple slices into "schnitz."

Missionaries and Indian traders preceded settlers in carrying apples into the wilderness. For the pioneers that followed, apples became an important source for food and barter. High penalties were imposed on those caught stealing apples.

One might conclude that the West Coast's introduction to apples came with the westward pioneer movement. On the contrary, apple seeds came around Cape Horn with a sea captain in the early 1800s. An Iowan, Henderson Luelling, later brought apple trees west to Oregon and established the first nursery on the Pacific coast.

However, John Chapman, better known as Johnny Appleseed, had more to do with the apple's increased popularity in America than perhaps any other individual. Traveling from New England with bags of apple seeds amongst his supplies, he planted orchards throughout the Ohio River valley wherever he found an appealing place. For 40 years he wandered over the countryside, clearing land for an orchard, fencing it, planting apple seeds, and moving on.

A number of varieties such as York, Winesap, Newtown, Northern Spy, Rhode Island Greening (Yellow Sweeting), and

Jonathans were developed prior to 1800 and are still eaten today. Other little-used types are no longer commercially profitable to raise. These can only be enjoyed visually at the "Old Variety Orchard" in Northgrafton, Massachusetts, where 50 rare species are preserved for their aesthetic and historical value.

How apples are produced: Because of cross-pollination, apples do not reproduce identical seeds. In other words, a tree grown from seed will not duplicate the fruit from which the seed originated. Thus, Hiatt discovered the Red Delicious apple in Peru, Iowa; Mullins of West Virginia came upon a Golden Delicious tree; and McIntosh named the McIntosh apple.

Through apple growing, the science of pomology, changes continue in tree size and shape as well as in fruit shape, color, and flavor. Replication of desirable varieties develops through budding and grafting, where live buds from the desired tree are attached to seedlings of still another variety.

Most apple trees begin to produce fruit within four or five years and continue doing so for 35 to 40 years. Today's top-quality fruit is a result of orchardists' efforts to manage the many tasks of planting, pruning, controlling insects and diseases, pollinating, thinning, harvesting, storing, packing, and marketing.

Nutritional value: There's no guarantee in that "apple a day keeps the doctor away" theory, but apples are a dietary asset. Although not outstandingly high in any one vitamin or mineral, apples supply carbohydrates for energy, yet one medium apple provides only about 90 calories.

Historically, Englishmen and Germans used apples to cure digestive problems. Apples' mild acidity and bulk are still known to aid digestion. Crisp raw apples, in addition, help cleanse the teeth.

Types of apples

Each apple variety in the markets and fruit stands has definite flavor—sweet, tart, mellow, piquant—and distinctive texture—crisp, juicy, mealy, hard, snappy. The color of the flesh can range from white to delicate yellow. The red, yellow, or green skin color can be dark, bright, mottled, or striped. One strain is such a dark red it almost looks black.

Each type of apple may have one or several uses. Some are best suited for eating out of hand, others best for making sauces, puddings, pies, or cobblers. In general, however, no hard and fast rule dictates which type of apple must be put to which use. Personal preferences and family favorites play an important part in this selection.

Apple use recommendations as given below are based on tests and majority opinions. Many people like the snap of a Baldwin for eating raw; some prefer the crisp juiciness of a McIntosh for all uses. The adjacent pictures identify the eight varieties most frequently seen in grocery stores and at roadside stands. Use them in conjunction with the apple use guide to identify the different varieties and to help solve the problem of which apples to use and choose.

Apples and their uses

Eating
   Baldwin, Golden Delicious, Jonathan, McIntosh, Northern Spy, Red Delicious, Stayman, Wealthy, Winesap

Baking
   Rhode Island Greening, Rome Beauty

Pie Making
   Baldwin, Golden Delicious, Jonathan, McIntosh, Northern Spy, Rhode Island Greening, Stayman, Wealthy, Winesap, York

Cooking
   Baldwin, Cortland, Jonathan, McIntosh, Northern Spy, Rhode Island Greening, Rome Beauty, Stayman, Wealthy, Winesap, Yellow Newtown, York

All-Purpose
   Baldwin, Jonathan, McIntosh, Northern Spy, Stayman, Wealthy, Winesap

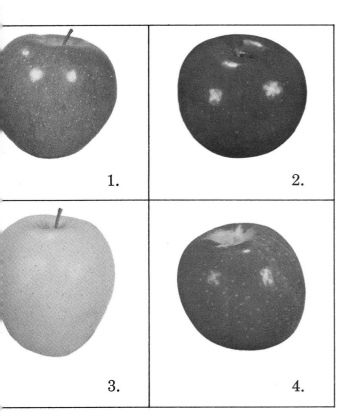

1. Rome Beauty—Red with red stripes. Has shallow "cup" around stem. Firm texture; mild flavor. Suggested for cooking and baking. Available throughout United States from November to June.

2. Stayman—Close relative to Winesap, but more elongated in shape. Rich red skin. Semi-firm texture; wine-like flavor. All-purpose apple grown in Eastern Appalachia area. Available November to March.

3. Golden Delicious—Yellow apple similar in shape and texture to Red Delicious. Tangy-sweet flavor. Good for eating out-of-hand, salads, sauce, and pies. Available from October to May.

4. York—Also called York Imperial. Red and green coloring; lopsided shape. Firm texture; tart and juicy flavor. Best for cooking and baking. Available from November through March in Southeast.

5. Winesap—One of oldest American varieties. Deep red color. Somewhat elongated yet oval shape. Firm texture; tart, wine-like flavor. All-purpose apple. Available throughout country from December to July.

6. McIntosh—Two-toned red and green skin; oval shape. Tender; rich, spicy, juicy taste and aromatic odor. An all-purpose apple. Grown mostly in eastern United States. Available September to May.

7. Jonathan—Bright red with green in some strains; oval shape. Tender texture; tart, juicy flavor. Eaten fresh or cooked. Grown mostly in Midwest. Available throughout from September to January.

8. Red Delicious—Bright red color. Identified by "broad shoulders" tapering to 5 nodules at base. Crisp texture; sweet flavor. A most popular eating apple. Available from late September to July.

How to select

At one time, apples were winter fruits. Today, thanks to modern methods of commercial storage in atmospherically controlled rooms, several varieties of apples are available the year around.

Although they can be bought in convenient plastic bags, in film-wrapped tray packs, or by the pound, peck, and bushel, buymanship involves choosing quality fruits that serve the desired function no matter what quantity purchased.

Apple selection depends first on their intended use. For eating out-of-hand, apples should be firm, juicy, and free of blemishes. For baking, the variety chosen should feel firm and hold its shape well when baked. Choose cooking apples that will cook tender in a short time.

How the apples are to be used determines what quantity of fruit to buy. Purchasing large amounts, for example by the bushel, will usually be more economical per pound than smaller units; but available storage and frequency of use must also be considered. The following guidelines can help in calculating the family's needs. There are about 3 medium-sized apples in a pound, about 40 in a peck, and about 150 in a bushel. One pound of unpeeled apples yields about 3 cups, peeled, diced, or sliced fruit for recipe use.

Quality is the second consideration in apple selection. Bright, sparkling color is one of the best guides to good apples. The "ground color" (green areas on red apples) should be greenish yellow. The darker and greener the ground color, the more immature the apple; texture will be hard and flavor probably poor. If the ground color is too yellow, the apple is overripe indicating poor flavor and mealy texture. A light russet (rough skin of reddish brown color) does not affect the tantalizing flavor or eating quality of apples.

Skin appearance is another quality indicator. The apples should look smooth and be reasonably free of bruises. Too many bruises or decay spots identify apples that are too ripe or have been handled roughly. But in testing the firmness of apples, don't pinch them—pinching may add another unwanted bruise.

Recent processing techniques include the application of a harmless wax to the apple exterior. The exceedingly good shine produced is easily recognized and should not be used as a guide to quality.

As another selection aid, the federal government has established specific grade standards for apples based on maturity, degree of ripeness, uniformity of size, color for the variety, and lack of or presence of admissible blemishes. Most states have also adopted these or similar grade standards for apples that come only under intrastate control.

The apple section of the produce counter or the apple container should be marked with some grade. The most familiar ones found are U.S. Extra Fancy and U.S. Fancy. An apple package labeled U.S. No. 1 meets minimum grading standards. A combination rating such as "Combination U.S. Extra Fancy and U.S. Fancy" may also be seen. As added insurance, check the apple grade before buying.

How to store

Although apples have fine keeping qualities, they need care to hold them at their peak. Gentle handling prevents bruises. Any apples with bruised or broken skins should be separated from those without defects and used promptly.

Storing apples purchased in bulk for homes use in a cool, preferably moist place enables them to stay fresh longer. Small quantities should be refrigerator-stored in a plastic bag which has a few perforated holes. These holes allow air into the bag so the apples can "breathe."

Apples need to be kept cold for best quality retention, but should not be stored near the freezer section as they may freeze. Serve apples chilled or at room temperature, as desired, but always keep the reserve supply refrigerated.

How to prepare

After careful buying and storing, those top quality apples chosen deserve the best handling in preparation. Basic techniques such as peeling, coring, and retaining good color are the groundwork for an appetizing dish. First, however, wash the apples thoroughly under cold water.

To peel or not to peel an apple depends primarily on personal preference and the intended use of the apple. The red or yellow skin can add appealing color to an otherwise lifeless salad or dessert, but some people prefer the flavor and texture of the peeled fruit. When a recipe calls for grated or shredded apple, peeling enhances the final appearance.

Spicy Fruit Puffs

> 2 cups sifted all-purpose flour
> 3 teaspoons baking powder
> ½ teaspoon ground cinnamon
> ¼ teaspoon ground nutmeg
> 1 cup shredded peeled apple
> ⅔ cup brown sugar
> ¼ cup chopped walnuts
> ⅔ cup milk
> 2 beaten eggs
> ¼ cup shortening, melted and cooled
> 1 cup whole wheat *or* bran flakes

Sift together first 4 ingredients and 1 teaspoon salt. Stir in apple, sugar, and nuts. Combine milk, eggs, and shortening; add all at once. Stir just to blend. Fold in cereal. Fill greased muffin pans ⅔ full. Bake at 400° for 15 to 20 minutes. Makes 12 muffins.

Sweet Apple Ring

Dissolve one 3-ounce package lemon-flavored gelatin in 1 cup boiling apple juice. Stir in 1 cup cold water and ¼ teaspoon salt; chill till partially set. Fold in one 8¾-ounce can pineapple tidbits, drained; ½ cup miniature marshmallows; ½ cup diced unpeeled apple; and ¼ cup seedless green grapes. Pour into 4½-cup ring mold. Chill till firm. Serves 4 or 5.

In most baked products, apples are peeled; but baked whole apples are left unpeeled so that the fruits retain their shape. Peeling a strip about a fourth or third of the way down is suggested to prevent the skins from cracking.

Spicy Baked Apples

Core six large baking apples and peel each about ¼ of the way down. Arrange 6 slices unpeeled orange in bottom of 10x6x1½-inch baking dish. Place an apple on each orange slice. Fill apple centers with mixture of ¾ cup snipped pitted dates, 3 tablespoons broken walnuts, and ½ teaspoon grated orange peel.*

In small saucepan combine 1 cup brown sugar, 1 cup water, 2 tablespoons butter or margarine, ½ teaspoon ground cinnamon, and ½ teaspoon ground nutmeg; bring to boiling. Pour hot syrup around apples. Bake uncovered at 350° for 50 to 60 minutes, basting occasionally. Serve warm with cream. Serves 6.

*Or, fill centers of apples with ½ cup prepared mincemeat. Bake as above.

Coring apples is a simple operation when the inexpensive apple corer is used. Insert the corer tip off-center in the apple. Push through the blossom end, then twist until the core is cut loose. Where the apple must be cored and cut further, another tool is available that cores and slices the apple in one operation.

When cut, apple flesh is very susceptible to browning. If they are not to be used immediately, treating the apple pieces with ascorbic acid color keeper following package directions, or dipping them in lemon or other fruit juice mixed with a little water, retards discoloration. Perfect for recipes using cut fresh apples is the Yellow Delicious apple. Its flesh will stay white longer than any other apple variety.

Because of their natural juices, apples need very little cooking water. Do *not* add water when making apple pies, cobblers, or betties and add only enough to applesauce to prevent scorching.

Careful addition of sugar highlights the natural apple flavor. The amount used depends first on the tartness of the apples, but too much sugar will hide the natural flavor and make the apples mushy.

How to use

The recipes which follow are evidence of the versatility of this fruit. Apples are equally delicious fresh, cooked, or

baked—used with cheese, meat, poultry. Serve them in the daily menu as appetizer, entrée, salad, dessert, or snack as desired. (See also *Fruit*.)

Cheese-Stuffed Apples

    1 3-ounce package cream cheese,
        softened
 1⅓ ounces camembert cheese
    1 tablespoon dry white wine
            . . .
    4 medium apples

Beat cheeses and wine with electric or rotary beater till smooth. Core apples; scoop out leaving shells about ½ inch thick. Fill with cheese. Chill 2 to 3 hours. Cut in wedges.

Caramel Apples

Melt one 14-ounce package (about 50) vanilla caramels with 2 tablespoons water in top of double boiler, stirring frequently till mixture is smooth. Add dash salt.

Stick a wooden skewer into each blossom end of 6 unpeeled, crisp medium apples. Dip apples in caramel syrup and turn until bottom halves of apples are completely coated. (If syrup is too stiff, add few drops water.)

At once roll bottoms of coated apples in chopped walnuts. Set on cookie sheet covered with waxed paper. Chill till caramel coating is firm. Top wooden skewers with large pieces of corn candy, if desired.

Apple-Peach Conserve

Combine 2 cups *each* chopped, peeled tart apples and chopped, peeled peaches; 3 cups sugar; and ⅓ cup lemon juice. Cook slowly for 20 minutes. Pour into hot scalded jars. Seal at once. Makes about four ½-pints.

America's most popular pie

← Perfect Apple Pie is equally delicious when topped with a standard pie crust or attractively dressed in sugary lattice work.

Apple-Orange Toss

Both tasty and easy to prepare—

    1 medium tart apple, diced
   ½ teaspoon shredded orange peel
    1 medium orange, peeled and
        diced
    2 tablespoons broken walnuts
   ¼ cup mayonnaise or salad
        dressing

Combine all ingredients; toss together lightly. Serve on lettuce, if desired. Serves 2 or 3.

Lemon Apple Salad

    1 3-ounce package lemon-flavored
        gelatin
   ½ cup dairy sour cream
    1 medium apple, peeled,
        quartered, cored, and
        grated (1 cup)

Dissolve gelatin in 1½ cups boiling water. Blend in sour cream. Chill till partially set. Fold in grated apple. Pour into 3½-cup ring mold. Chill till firm. Makes 4 or 5 servings.

Apple Snow Salad

A freezer recipe—

    1 8¾-ounce can crushed
        pineapple, undrained
    2 beaten eggs
   ½ cup sugar
   ¼ cup water
    3 tablespoons lemon juice
      Dash salt
    2 cups diced unpeeled apple
   ½ cup chopped walnuts
    1 cup whipping cream

In saucepan combine first 6 ingredients. Cook over low heat, stirring constantly, till thickened. Chill thoroughly.

Stir in apple and nuts. Whip cream till soft peaks form; fold into apple mixture. Pour into 8x8x2-inch pan. Freeze till firm. Let stand at room temperature 10 to 15 minutes before serving. Cut into squares. Serves 9.

Caramel-sauced pecan halves garnish a glistening Topsy-Turvy Apple Pie—a scrumptious pie with an upside-down twist.

Apple Ring Waldorf

    1 3-ounce package lemon-flavored
         gelatin
    1 medium unpeeled apple
          • • •
    2 teaspoons lemon juice
    ½ cup miniature marshmallows
    ½ cup mayonnaise or salad
         dressing
    ⅓ cup chopped celery
    2 tablespoons chopped walnuts

Prepare gelatin following package directions; chill till partially set. Pour a little gelatin into 6½-cup ring mold. Cut enough thin apple wedges to fit bottom of mold; lay wedges with unpeeled side out around outside edge of mold. Chill till *almost* firm.

Dice remaining apple; sprinkle with lemon juice and fold into remaining gelatin. Fold in remaining ingredients. Spoon atop first layer. Chill till firm. Makes 6 servings.

Sausage-Stuffed Apples

    ½ pound bulk pork sausage
    ¼ cup chopped onion
    4 large baking apples
    ¼ cup finely crushed saltine
         crackers (7 crackers)
    1 beaten egg

Break up sausage in skillet; cook slowly with onion till meat is browned. Drain off fat. Core apples. Scoop out pulp leaving shells ½ inch thick; reserve pulp. Peel shells ¼ of the way down. Chop reserved pulp (about 1¼ cups); add to meat with crumbs, egg, ¼ teaspoon salt, and dash pepper; mix well.

Stuff apples with meat mixture. Bake at 375° for 40 minutes or till tender. Serves 4.

Apple-Tuna Toss

    1 medium head lettuce, torn in
         bite-size pieces (4 cups)
    2 cups diced unpeeled apple
    1 11-ounce can mandarin oranges,
         drained
    1 6½- or 7-ounce can tuna, drained
         and broken in chunks
    ⅓ cup coarsely chopped walnuts
    ½ cup mayonnaise
    2 teaspoons soy sauce
    1 teaspoon lemon juice

In large salad bowl combine first 5 ingredients. Combine mayonnaise, soy sauce, and lemon juice; mix well. Toss dressing lightly with salad mixture. Makes 4 to 6 servings.

Carrot-Apple-Ham Bake

Simmer 4 large carrots, peeled and sliced crosswise (2 cups), in salted water for 10 minutes; drain. In 2-quart casserole layer carrots; 4 cooking apples, peeled and thickly sliced (4 cups); and ¼ cup brown sugar. Dot with 1 tablespoon butter or margarine.

Combine ½ cup soft bread crumbs, ¼ cup milk, and 1 beaten egg. Add 2 cups ground fully cooked ham and mix well. Shape into 8 patties. Brown patties with hot shortening in skillet. Lay patties atop apples. Bake, covered, at 350° for 45 minutes. Makes 4 servings.

Apple Turkey Sandwiches

    4 slices buttered toast
    4 large slices cooked turkey
  ½ cup coarsely shredded, peeled,
      cored tart apple
  ½ cup mayonnaise
  ⅓ cup finely chopped celery
  ¼ cup snipped green onions with
      tops
  ½ to 1 teaspoon curry powder
  ¼ teaspoon salt

Arrange toast on baking sheet. Cover with turkey; sprinkle with salt and pepper to taste. Combine remaining ingredients and dash pepper; spread over turkey. Broil 7 to 8 inches from heat for 5 to 8 minutes or till heated through and lightly browned. Makes 4 servings.

Maple Baked Apples

Peel top half of 6 large tart red apples; remove cores. Place in 11x7x1½-inch baking dish. Combine 1 cup maple-flavored syrup and 2 teaspoons grated lemon peel. Pour over apples. Bake at 375° for 1 hour, basting apples with sauce frequently. Serve warm with cream or ice cream. Makes 6 servings.

Perfect Apple Pie

    6 to 8 tart apples, peeled, cored,
      and thinly sliced (6 cups)*
  ¾ to 1 cup sugar
    2 tablespoons all-purpose flour
  ½ to 1 teaspoon ground cinnamon
      Dash ground nutmeg
      Plain Pastry for 2-crust 9-inch
      pie (See *Pastry*)
    2 tablespoons butter or margarine

If apples lack tartness, sprinkle with about 1 tablespoon lemon juice. Combine sugar, flour, cinnamon, nutmeg, and dash salt; mix with apples. Line 9-inch pie plate with pastry. Fill with apple mixture; dot with butter. Adjust top crust, cutting slits for escape of steam; seal. Sprinkle with sugar. Bake at 400° for 50 minutes or till done.

*Or, use two 20-ounce cans (about 5 cups) pie-sliced apples, drained.

Topsy-Turvy Apple Pie

  ¼ cup butter or margarine,
      softened
  ½ cup pecan halves
  ½ cup brown sugar
      Plain Pastry for 2-crust 9-inch
      pie (See *Pastry*)
    5 large tart apples, peeled,
      cored, and sliced (about 6
      cups)
    1 tablespoon lemon juice
  ½ cup sugar
    1 tablespoon all-purpose flour
  ½ teaspoon ground cinnamon
  ½ teaspoon ground nutmeg

Spread butter evenly on bottom and sides of 9-inch pie plate. Press nuts, rounded side down, into butter on bottom of plate. Pat brown sugar evenly over nuts. Roll out pastry for bottom crust; place in pie plate over sugar.

Sprinkle apples with lemon juice. Combine flour, cinnamon, nutmeg, and dash salt; toss with apples. Turn into pie plate; spread evenly to keep top level. Roll out remaining pastry; adjust over apples and seal. Prick top of pie with fork. Bake at 400° for 50 minutes.

Remove from oven; cool 5 minutes. Place serving plate atop pie; invert. Carefully remove pie plate. Serve warm or cool.

Apple Crumb Pie

      Plain Pastry for 1-crust 9-inch
      pie (See *Pastry*)
    5 to 7 tart apples, peeled,
      cored, and cut in
      eighths (5 cups)
  ½ cup sugar
  ¾ teaspoon ground cinnamon
  ¾ cup all-purpose flour
  ⅓ cup sugar
    6 tablespoons butter or margarine

Line 9-inch pie plate with pastry. Arrange apples in unbaked shell. Mix the ½ cup sugar and cinnamon; sprinkle over apples.

Mix flour with the ⅓ cup sugar; cut in butter till crumbly. Sprinkle over apples. Bake at 400° for 35 to 40 minutes or till done. (If pie browns too quickly, cover edge with foil.) Cool. Pass whipped cream, if desired.

Apple Custard Pie

     Plain Pastry for 1-crust 9-inch
        pie (See *Pastry*)
 6 to 8 tart apples, peeled, cored,
        and cut in eighths (6 cups)
  ¾ cup sugar
   3 tablespoons all-purpose flour
  ¼ cup light cream
     Ground cinnamon

Line 9-inch pie plate with pastry. Arrange apples in unbaked shell. Combine sugar, flour, and ½ teaspoon salt; stir in cream. Pour mixture over apples. Sprinkle with cinnamon.

Cover pie loosely with foil. Bake at 375° for 1 hour. Remove foil; bake 15 minutes more or till apples are done. Serve warm with slices of Cheddar cheese, if desired.

Apple-Raisin Pie

A hint of rum enhances the fruit combination—

  ¾ cup sugar
   2 tablespoons all-purpose flour
   1 cup raisins
 3 to 4 tart apples*, peeled,
        cored, and thinly sliced
   2 tablespoons rum
     Plain Pastry for 2-crust 9-inch
        pie (See *Pastry*)
   3 slices sharp process American
        cheese

In saucepan blend sugar, flour and ¼ teaspoon salt; stir in ½ cup water and raisins. Cook, stirring constantly, till mixture thickens, about 5 minutes. Add apples and rum.

Line 9-inch pie plate with pastry; fill with apple mixture. Adjust top crust over filling; seal. Cut slits in top crust. Sprinkle with sugar, if desired. Gently fold a strip of foil around rim of crust covering fluted edge. (This guards against boil-over and overbrowning.)

Bake at 400° for 40 to 50 minutes or till done. Before serving, top pie with 6 triangles of cheese; broil to melt cheese. Serve warm.

*If apples lack tartness, sprinkle slices with 1 tablespoon lemon juice. *Or* use one 20-ounce can (2½ cups) pie-sliced apples. Drain apples, *reserving liquid*. Use apple liquid in place of water for plumping raisins.

Mock Mince Pie

 1⅓ cups sugar
  ½ teaspoon salt
  ½ teaspoon ground cinnamon
  ¼ teaspoon ground cloves
  ¼ teaspoon ground ginger
 1½ cups finely chopped peeled
        apples
   1 cup raisins
  ½ cup canned jellied cranberry
        sauce, broken up
  ⅓ cup coarsely chopped walnuts
   1 teaspoon grated orange peel
  ½ teaspoon grated lemon peel
  ¼ cup lemon juice
     Plain Pastry for 2-crust 9-inch
        pie (See *Pastry*)
     Butter or margarine

In bowl mix together sugar, salt, cinnamon, cloves, and ginger. Add fruit, nuts, orange and lemon peel, and lemon juice; mix well.

Line 9-inch pie plate with pastry; fill with apple mixture. Dot with butter. Adjust top crust over filling; seal. Cut slits in top. Bake at 400° for 30 to 35 minutes or till browned. Serve warm. Top each serving with shredded or thinly sliced Cheddar or sharp process American cheese, if desired.

For Apple Dumplings, pastry squares are traditionally folded to the centers of the sugar-and-spice apples then pinched together.

Apple Dumplings

2¼ cups sifted all-purpose flour
½ teaspoon salt
⅔ cup shortening, chilled
6 to 8 tablespoons cold water
6 small apples, peeled and cored
⅔ cup granulated sugar
¼ cup light cream
¾ cup *hot* maple *or* maple-blended syrup
6 tablespoons butter or margarine, softened
1 cup sifted confectioners' sugar *or* 1 cup brown *or* maple sugar

In bowl mix flour and salt. Cut in shortening till mixture resembles coarse crumbs. Sprinkle water over a little at a time; mix lightly till all is moistened. Form into ball; roll out on lightly floured surface to 18x12-inch rectangle; cut into six 6-inch squares.

Place an apple in center of each square. Mix the ⅔ cup sugar and cream; spoon into centers of apples. Moisten edges of pastry; fold corners to center. Pinch edges together.

Place 1 inch apart in ungreased 11x7x1½-inch baking pan. Bake at 450° for 15 minutes. Reduce oven temperature to 350°. Baste apples with hot maple syrup. Return to oven and bake 30 minutes longer or till apples are done, basting with hot maple syrup every 15 minutes.

Serve with additional hot maple syrup or *Hard Sauce:* Cream butter with confectioners' sugar till fluffy. Drop from teaspoon onto waxed paper making 6 mounds. Sprinkle generously with ground nutmeg; chill. Serves 6.

Apple Crisp

5 to 6 cups peeled, cored, thinly sliced apples
¾ cup quick-cooking rolled oats
¾ cup brown sugar
½ cup all-purpose flour
¼ teaspoon ground cinnamon
½ cup butter or margarine

Arrange apples in greased 8x1½-inch round pan. Combine oats, sugar, flour, and cinnamon; cut into butter. Sprinkle mixture over apples. Bake at 350° for 35 to 40 minutes. Serve warm with cream, if desired. Makes 6 servings.

Apple-Oatmeal Cookies

1 cup finely diced unpeeled apple
¼ cup raisins
¼ cup chopped pecans
½ cup granulated sugar
. . .
1 cup butter or margarine
1 cup brown sugar
2 eggs
. . .
2 cups sifted all-purpose flour
2 teaspoons baking powder
1 teaspoon ground cinnamon
½ teaspoon salt
½ teaspoon ground cloves
½ cup milk
2 cups quick-cooking rolled oats

In saucepan combine apple, raisins, nuts, the ½ cup sugar, and 2 tablespoons water. Cook and stir till mixture is thick and apples are tender, about 10 minutes. Cream butter and brown sugar till fluffy. Beat in eggs. Sift together flour, baking powder, cinnamon, salt, and cloves; add alternately with milk to creamed mixture. Stir in rolled oats.

Reserve ¾ cup dough. Drop remainder from teaspoon onto greased cookie sheet; make depressions in centers; top each with apple filling and dab of reserved dough. Bake at 375° for 10 to 12 minutes. Makes 36.

Apple products

Controlled-atmosphere storage, as previously noted, has been one contributing factor in the growth of year-round apple popularity. The development of commercially-produced apple products, like applesauce and apple juice, has also shared in this expansion. But this market has taken a long time to develop. While experiments in canning apples were conducted in the 1800s, processing in commercial amounts did not succeed until the 1920s arrived. Today, more than one-third of the apple crop is sold for a variety of processing purposes.

The canning technique has also been influenced by the type of product desired. Each product requires a special apple variety or varieties that retains certain flavor and texture characteristics. Firm, crisp apple varieties are suited for canning apple

slices while apples with totally different characteristics are selected for apple butter or dried apple slices.

In addition to the processed products, many commercial by-products are extracted from apple pulp, skins, seeds, and cores. Pectin, vinegar, apple pomace, and even volatile flavors are only a few.

At home, many apple products can be prepared on a smaller-than-commercial scale. Some families prefer applesauce made from a specific variety which is not available commercially. Some want to take advantage of the backyard tree which is full of fruit. Whether purchased or homemade, these apple-based foods make tasteful menu additions.

Apple Butter: A traditional Pennsylvania-Dutch fruit spread. Cut-up apples or apple pulp are cooked with apple cider and spices to a thick dark paste. Years ago, large batches were made in a huge crock in the oven of a coal stove. Several days were needed for thickening.

Now many manufacturers market apple butter commercially. No longer considered just a spread, it can be a pleasing sweet accompaniment or a recipe ingredient. (See also *Fruit Butter.*)

Apple Butter

Core and quarter 6 pounds of unpeeled tart apples; cook with 6 cups apple cider *or* apple juice in large heavy saucepan till soft, about 30 minutes. Press through food mill. Boil gently 30 minutes, stirring occasionally.

Stir in 3 cups sugar, 2 teaspoons ground cinnamon, and ½ teaspoon ground cloves. Cook and stir over low heat till sugar dissolves. Boil gently, stirring frequently, till desired thickness, about 1 hour. Pour into 8 hot ½-pint jars; adjust lids and process in boiling water bath for 10 minutes (start counting time after water returns to boil).

A moist, delicious cake

←Spice, swirl, and spread Apple Butter Cake with homemade or commercial apple butter. Unpeeled apple wedges trim the sides.

Apple Butter Cake

    ½ cup shortening
    1 cup sugar
    3 eggs
 1½ cups apple butter
 2½ cups sifted cake flour
    3 teaspoons baking powder
    ½ teaspoon baking soda
    ½ teaspoon salt
    ½ teaspoon ground cinnamon
    ¼ teaspoon ground nutmeg
    1 cup sour milk
    1 recipe Seven-minute Frosting
      (See *Frosting*)

Cream together shortening and sugar. Beat in eggs, one at a time; beat till light and fluffy. Stir in *1 cup* apple butter. Sift together flour, baking powder, baking soda, salt, cinnamon, and nutmeg. Add flour mixture to creamed mixture alternately with sour milk.

Turn batter into 2 greased and lightly floured 9x1½-inch round pans. Bake at 350° for 30 to 35 minutes. Cool 10 minutes. Remove from pans; cool layers thoroughly.

Spread one layer of cooled cake with ¼ *cup* of remaining apple butter. Top with *1 cup* Seven-minute Frosting, spreading evenly to cover apple butter. Cover with second cake layer. Frost sides and top of cake with remaining Seven-minute Frosting. Swirl remaining ¼ cup apple butter on frosted top to give marbled effect. If desired, garnish sides of cake with unpeeled apple wedges.

Apple Cider: Sweet (unfermented) or hard (fermented) apple juice. The indiscriminate use of the word "cider" often refers to a number of different products. The "cider" found in grocery outlets is usually pure unfermented apple juice that has been pasteurized. In hard or fermented cider (often sold at roadside stands, all the sugar has been converted to alcohol. (See also *Cider.*)

Applejack: The Americanized word for apple brandy. Applejack is primarily prepared today by distilling hard cider.

Years ago American colonists developed their own more interesting process. First the apple juice was fermented to the highest alcoholic content. The resulting hard cider was then left to freeze. As alcohol freezes at a considerably lower temperature than water, the water in the cider froze. The remaining liquid, now the pure alcohol called applejack, was drawn or skimmed off.

Juices like cider or applejack, were favorite alcoholic beverages of early Americans, particularly in rural areas. This country's forefathers firmly believed that strong spirits like applejack were helpful to maintain good health. It was not uncommon for the head of the household to have a stiff boost of applejack for breakfast. With jug in hand, he then went to work in the field. Applejack made frequent appearances at social events, too.

Although applejack is an American term, apple brandy is made in other parts of the world. Most famous and perhaps the finest apple brandy comes from Calvados, in Normandy, France. (See also *Brandy*.)

Apple Juice: Unsweetened pressed juice of apples. The freshly pressed juice is treated at controlled temperatures to prevent the growth of naturally occurring yeasts and molds that would otherwise cause the juice to ferment.

There are two types of this unfermented apple juice; nonclarified and clarified. The process for nonclarified juice removes only the heavy apple pulp in the liquid; the beverage is slightly cloudy. Clarified juice is passed through very fine filters to produce a perfectly clear liquid.

Both types of apple juice have delicate apple flavor and the same nutritive value. Apple juice is usually used as a pleasant fruit drink or as the liquid in gelled salads where apple flavor is desired. (See also *Fruit Juice*.)

Apple-Lime Cooler

A soothing refresher in hot summer—

Beat ½ pint lime sherbet with a rotary beater till softened and smooth. Gradually stir in ¾ cup chilled apple juice till mixture is blended. Pour sherbet mixture into chilled glasses; serve at once. Makes 2 servings.

Apple Blush

4 cups apple juice *or* apple cider
1 12-ounce can (1½ cups) apricot
   nectar
½ cup lemon juice
¼ cup grenadine syrup
1 28-fluid ounce bottle ginger
   ale, chilled
1 pint lemon sherbet

Combine apple juice, apricot nectar, lemon juice, and grenadine; chill. Pour over ice in punch bowl. Resting bottle on rim, slowly add soda. Float scoops of sherbet. Makes 9½ cups.

Apple Pie Filling: A general term for canned apple slices used mostly in pies but also usable as an ingredient in a variety of recipes.

Two main kinds of apple pie filling are produced. In the first type, often called pie-sliced apples, the apples are unsweetened and packed in their own juice. No thickening agent is present. Other ingredients are needed before the slices can be successfully used. The apple slices in the second type of pie filling are canned with

Apple pie filling is purchasable in several forms: French apple pie filling, plain apple pie filling, and pie-sliced apples.

a sweet, thick sauce. In this form the product is ready to use without the addition of other ingredients. (See also *Pie Filling.*)

Creamy Apple-Cheese Bake

    1 cup sifted all-purpose flour
    1 tablespoon sugar
    ¼ cup butter or margarine
    1 slightly beaten egg yolk
            • • •
    1 20-ounce can pie-sliced apples,
        drained
    ⅓ cup sugar
    1 teaspoon lemon juice
    ¼ teaspoon ground cinnamon
    ¼ teaspoon ground nutmeg
            • • •
    ½ cup sugar
    2 slightly beaten eggs
    1 4-ounce container *whipped*
        cream cheese
    ½ cup whipping cream
    1 teaspoon vanilla

To prepare crust combine flour, the 1 tablespoon sugar, and dash salt. Finely cut in butter. Combine the 1 egg yolk with 1 teaspoon water; blend into crumb mixture. Press on bottom and sides of 8x8x2-inch baking pan.

To prepare filling combine apples, the ⅓ cup sugar, lemon juice, cinnamon, and nutmeg. Turn into crust; bake at 425° for 10 minutes.

Meanwhile, mix the ½ cup sugar, 2 eggs, cheese, and dash salt. Blend in cream and vanilla. Pour over apples. Bake at 350° for 30 to 35 minutes or till knife inserted off-center comes out clean. Makes 8 or 9 servings.

Curried Apple Relish

    2 tablespoons butter or margarine
    1 teaspoon sugar
    ½ teaspoon curry powder
    1 20-ounce can pie-sliced
        apples, drained

Melt butter in skillet. Stir in sugar and curry. Add apples; toss to coat. Cook over low heat, stirring occasionally, till apples are heated through, about 5 minutes. Serve with meat or poultry. Makes 6 to 8 servings.

Date Apple Torte

    1 21-ounce can apple pie filling
    1 teaspoon grated orange peel
    2 tablespoons orange juice
            • • •
    1 14-ounce package date bar mix
    ½ cup chopped walnuts
    1 egg

Spread pie filling in 9x9x2-inch baking pan. Sprinkle orange peel over; pour orange juice over all. Prepare date filling from date bar mix according to package directions. Stir in nuts. Add crumbly mixture from bar mix and egg; blend. Spread over apples. Bake at 375° for 35 to 40 minutes. Serve with cream or ice cream, if desired. Makes 6 servings.

Apple Rings: Accompaniments or garnishes made from horizontal slices of cored apple. Jars of spiced rings can be purchased. Rings made at home are peeled or unpeeled, according to choice, and used raw, spiced, sautéed, or glazed.

Raw apple rings should be kept in a bowl of water mixed with a little ascorbic acid color keeper or lemon juice until used.

To prepare apple rings core peeled or unpeeled apple. Slice to desired thickness. Keep bright with ascorbic acid color keeper.

For cooked rings, firm apples such as Baldwins or Jonathans are usually chosen so that the rings retain their shape. (See *Accompaniment, Garnish* for additional information.)

Cinnamon Apple Rings

½ cup red cinnamon candies
¼ cup sugar
3 medium apples (1 pound)

In skillet combine cinnamon candies, sugar, and 2 cups water. Stir over medium heat till sugar and candies are dissolved. Core apples; cut crosswise in ½-inch rings. Add rings to syrup. Simmer gently till transparent but not soft. Cool rings in syrup.

Applesauce: A sweetened sauce made from cooked apples. At first applesauce was a simple dish prepared by cooking apple pieces until they were tender, then straining. But applesauce has become a made-to-order product. Some people like it smooth, others chunky. Some even prefer the apple slices left whole in a syrup.

No matter how homemade applesauce is prepared, tart juicy apples are the best type to use for both flavor and texture. The color may be creamy yellow or pink. Pink strained applesauce is made by using unpeeled red-skinned apples.

Applesauce

Chunky: Peel, core, and slice 4 medium apples. Combine 1 cup water, ¼ cup sugar, and dash ground mace; bring to boil. Add apples; cover and simmer till tender, about 8 minutes.

Smooth: Peel, core, and quarter 4 medium apples. Combine apples, ¼ to ½ cup water, and 2 inches stick cinnamon. Cover and simmer till very tender, 10 minutes. Remove cinnamon. Mash apples till smooth. Stir in ¼ cup sugar. (For larger quantity, don't peel apples; put cooked sauce through food mill or sieve.)

Blender: Peel, core, and cube 4 medium apples. Put ¼ cup water and 2 tablespoons lemon juice into blender container. Add cubed apples, ¼ cup sugar, and 1 tablespoon red cinnamon

Presenting a few of the wide array of processed apple products: apple butter and two kinds of applesauce—plain and raspberry.

candies (*or* 5 to 6 drops red food coloring). Cover and blend till smooth. Serve immediately, or transfer to saucepan and bring to boiling to keep apples from darkening.

On the grocers' shelves applesauce, the number one processed apple product, is seen in a number of forms. It is available plain in cans or jars. Although usually a blend of from two to five apple varieties, certain brands use one kind of apples exclusively. There's applesauce with chunks of apple, pink applesauce with a blend of raspberries, and another with cranberries.

Quick Applesauce Crisp

An easy dessert for unexpected company—

Combine one 16-ounce can applesauce, ½ cup brown sugar, ¼ cup raisins, and ½ teaspoon ground cinnamon; pour into 8¼x1¾-inch round baking dish. Combine 1 cup packaged biscuit mix and ½ cup granulated sugar; cut in ¼ cup butter till crumbly. Add ¼ cup chopped walnuts. Sprinkle over mixture. Bake at 375° for 30 to 35 minutes. Serves 6.

Prepare applesauce any one of three ways—
for big golden chunks, cook the apple slices
only until they are tender.

Smooth applesauce is attained by cooking
apple slices till very tender, then mashing them smooth with a potato masher.

Blender applesauce is often served uncooked. If not to be used immediately, cook
it slightly to retain good color.

Applesauce is a versatile food. It's a
deliciously refreshing dessert for children
and adults. Serve as is with a cookie, or
add a garnish like whipped cream, a maraschino cherry, or bits of candied ginger.
Serve it hot as a sauce for warm ginger-
bread or sponge cake. Let it become a good-
tasting accompaniment to pork, duckling,
or goose. Applesauce is also a popular ingredient in a number of desserts as in traditional Applesauce Cake.

Applesauce Cake

   ½ cup butter or margarine
   2 cups sugar
   2 eggs
2½ cups sifted all-purpose flour
1½ teaspoons baking soda
   1 teaspoon salt
   1 teaspoon ground cinnamon
   ½ teaspoon ground nutmeg
   ¼ teaspoon ground allspice
1½ cups canned applesauce
   ½ cup raisins
   ½ cup chopped pecans

Cream butter; gradually add sugar creaming
till light and fluffy. Add eggs, one at a time,
beating well after each addition. Sift together
flour, baking soda, salt, cinnamon, nutmeg,
and allspice. Add flour mixture to creamed mixture alternately with applesauce.
   Stir raisins and pecans into batter. Turn batter into greased and lightly floured 13x9x2-inch
pan. Bake at 350° about 45 minutes or till
done. Cool cake in pan.

Applesauce Meat Loaf

    1 cup soft bread crumbs
    ½ cup applesauce
    1 pound ground beef
    1 slightly beaten egg
    2 tablespoons finely chopped
       onion
    1 teaspoon dried celery flakes
    2 teaspoons Dijon-style mustard
    ½ teaspoon salt
    ½ cup applesauce
    1 tablespoon brown sugar
    1 tablespoon vinegar

Combine bread crumbs with the first ½ cup applesauce. Add beef, egg, onion, celery flakes, *1 teaspoon* mustard, salt, and dash pepper; blend thoroughly. Shape into round loaf in 9x9x2-inch baking pan. With bowl of spoon make a depression in top of loaf.

    Combine remaining ½ cup applesauce, brown sugar, vinegar, and remaining mustard; pour into depression in meat loaf. Bake at 350° for 1 hour. Makes 4 or 5 servings.

Diamond Applesauce Brownies

    1 cup brown sugar
    6 tablespoons butter or margarine
    ½ cup applesauce
    1 beaten egg
    1 teaspoon shredded orange peel
    1 teaspoon vanilla
  1¼ cups sifted all-purpose flour
    1 teaspoon baking powder
    ½ teaspoon salt
    ¼ teaspoon baking soda
    ½ cup chopped walnuts

In saucepan combine brown sugar and butter. Cook and stir over medium heat till butter melts; remove from heat. Beat in applesauce, egg, orange peel, and vanilla. Sift together flour, baking powder, salt, and baking soda; stir into applesauce mixture. Stir in nuts.

    Spread mixture in greased 15½x10½x1-inch jelly roll pan. Bake at 350° about 15 minutes. While warm top with *Orange Glaze:* Combine 1½ cups sifted confectioners' sugar, ½ teaspoon vanilla, dash salt, and enough orange juice (about 2 tablespoons) to make mixture of glaze consistency. Cut in diamonds or bars.

Big Apple Parfaits

Combine 1¼ cups boiling water and one 3-ounce package raspberry-flavored gelatin; stir till gelatin is dissolved. Add one 16-ounce can applesauce and 2 tablespoons lemon juice. Chill till gelatin is partially set. Beat 2 egg whites with dash salt till soft peaks form. Gradually add ¼ cup sugar, beating till stiff peaks form. Fold into gelatin mixture.

    Alternately spoon gelatin mixture and vanilla ice cream into parfait glasses. Top each with whipped cream. Serve at once. Serves 6.

Applesauce Doughnuts

Blend 1 tablespoon shortening with ¾ cup brown sugar; stir in ½ cup applesauce and 1 egg. Sift together 2 cups sifted all-purpose flour, ½ teaspoon baking soda, and ¼ teaspoon *each* salt, ground cinnamon, and ground nutmeg. Gradually stir into applesauce mixture.

    Roll ½ inch thick on lightly floured surface. Cut with doughnut cutter. Fry in deep hot fat (365°) till browned, about 3 minutes. Drain; roll in cinnamon-sugar mixture. Makes 12.

Apple Cinnamon Crunch

    1 8-ounce can applesauce
    3 tablespoons red cinnamon
       candies
    4 or 5 drops red food coloring
    1 quart vanilla ice cream,
       softened
    1 14½-ounce package cinnamon
       streusel coffee cake mix
    1 21-ounce can apple pie filling
    1 tablespoon lemon juice

Combine applesauce, candies, and food coloring. Heat till candy is dissolved; cool. Stir into ice cream. Freeze 6 hours or overnight.

    Thoroughly combine topping mix and cake mix from cinnamon streusel coffee cake mix. Lightly press *half* the mixture into bottom of greased 9x9x2-inch baking pan. Spread apple pie filling over; sprinkle with lemon juice.

    Top with remaining dry mixture. Sprinkle ¼ cup water evenly over topping. Bake, uncovered, at 375° for 35 to 40 minutes. Cut in squares. Top with scoop of ice cream mixture. Serves 9.

APPLE MINT—A variety of mint with distinctive apple aroma. Easily grown in home herb gardens, apple mint with its delicate, pleasant smell is a desirable addition to many dishes such as mint tea, fruit combinations, and fruit salads. (See also *Mint*.)

APPLIANCE—A household apparatus, portable or nonportable, designed for a specific use or uses. Today's appliances are kitchen helpers par excellence. They let the homemaker cook wherever she wants to, indoors or out, in the kitchen or on the dining-room table. They provide a substitute for arm power, give essential or extra cooking facilities, and bring "cool cooking" to hot weather. They're real working partners, performing a multitude of tasks at the homemaker's command.

The expansion of home appliances has been one of the most significant trends in the last 50 years. Before that time, domestic help or the homemaker herself performed many of the tasks appliances do now. When a two-slice electric toaster with drop-down sides and a single-element hot plate came into the kitchen, no one dreamed of the long succession of appliances to follow. The hot plate became more efficient, the electric percolator appeared, and the convenience pattern of use was established and accepted.

Regardless of major appliances owned, estimates show that today the average family has ten portable appliances—either gas or electric. In the upcoming future more cordless appliances will appear. Even today, enticing sales-counter displays include an increasing number of appliances equipped with solid-state controls (as in the transistor radio) that can maintain high-speed performance.

It's probably correct that no homemaker needs all the appliances that are on the market. In order to sort through them all, proper selection, care, and operation can mean the difference between a piece of equipment that is used to the fullest extent or one that is pushed to the back of a cupboard or counter, then forgotten.

How to select: Price, trade name, guarantee, and service play a large part in appliance purchases. How the appliance is made and performs is the first buying factor to consider. Ponder questions like, "Which appliances are necessities, which will be used most often, and which will be just fun to have? How many jobs does each appliance perform? Is there convenient storage space available?" It's important to be critically practical.

Learn all about the appliance's construction, appearance, and safety *before* it's been purchased by reading the instruction booklet. The basic materials used, sturdiness, and finishing touches can be determined when you look the appliance over at the store or at home when specification sheets and manuals are scrutinized.

Inspect the appliance all around—front, rear, and sides. Materials used on the front and back may differ. Quality materials are non-corrosive, smooth. Make sure that surfaces are easy to clean; corners rounded; hinges, doors, latches, and controls are easy to reach, read, or control. Electrical safety may call for double insulation and the use of plastic or paint rather than metal and chrome. The finish used must be practical, safe, and comfortable, as well as pleasing to the eye.

In determining the desired style, a well-balanced product in form, color, and overall appearance is essential. Extremes in style are tiresome and can present redecorating problems. The appliance should be functional but graceful, too.

Manufacturers' model lines usually include a top, middle, and bottom quality range. Top models usually have more decorative trim in addition to having special features. The word "deluxe" on an appliance, however, does not necessarily indicate the best quality but can simply be the name of one style in the line.

Several standards and seals of quality can help the purchaser pick the most desirable and safest appliance. A product given ASA or American Standards Association approval meets qualifications established by this organization concerning composition, construction, tolerances, safety, performance, and use. Most major and some minor appliances are tested by ASA.

The Underwriters' Laboratory (UL) Seal seen on appliances says that the unit has been tested for fire, casualty, and electrical safety. The seal is usually found on the name plate but may be attached to the cord or body of the appliance. While not a guarantee, the UL seal is a reliable indication of product safety.

The gas and electric industries concern themselves with standards. For example, the American Gas Association places a star-shaped seal on gas-operated appliances which meet performance, structural, and safety requirements. Also, the National Electrical Manufacturers Association supplies members with quality standards.

Other organizations and companies have established their own testing programs. These approvals may also be indicated on the appliance, its labels, or tags. If uncertain about a particular testing program or certification, ask about the group sponsoring the test as well as just what the approval includes.

How to use: Thoroughly read the use and care booklet that comes with each appliance and become familiar with the information it includes. Discover how to handle the appliance for best performance, how to care for it properly. Appliances with special features often require special care. For example, specific cooking and cleaning techniques must be used with treated coatings such as some nonstick linings. Cordless appliances must be charged properly. Operating a self-cleaning oven is no difficult task when the "how to's" have been gleaned from the instruction booklet. Moreover, keep a file of all appliance bulletins, guarantees, and instruction booklets so that if problems concerning operation or servicing of an appliance arise, the information is readily available.

When appliances are stored in handy locations the homemaker soon learns their versatility. Attachments that fit onto mixers or blenders or even separate power units give extra mileage, too. These are the shredders, ice crushers, food choppers, can openers, knife sharpeners, meat grinders, juicers, and silver buffers.

With concentrated effort in careful selection and care, appliances can bring years of satisfaction and enjoyment to an already enjoyable area—the cooking world. (See also *Equipment.*)

APRICOT—The small, yellowish orange fruit of a temperate-zone tree. This fruit resembles both the peach and plum in flavor. The apricot is round to oval and has a single smooth, winged pit. A distinguishing deep cleft starts at the stem end of the apricot. The flowers of the apricot tree are white when in full bloom and are borne singly or doubly at a node.

Botanists once thought the apricot was native to Armenia in western Asia. Today evidence points to China where the tree still grows wild, and writings dated before 2,000 B.C. indicate it was being cultivated. The ancient world ascribed prophetic powers to the fruit. Confucius is said to have composed proverbs under an apricot tree, and Persian poets called the apricot "the seed of the Sun."

Apricots were known in Europe and England before 1500. The Spanish are credited with bringing the fruit to the New World. The trees prospered in sections of Mexico, and apricots were among the fruits to reach California with missionaries early in the 18th century.

Nutritional value: Raw apricots are a fair source and dried apricots are a good source of vitamin A. Seventeen dried apricot halves give twice the recommended daily allowance of vitamin A, while two fresh apricots give half of this recommended allowance. In three medium fresh apricots there are 54 calories and four large dried apricot halves yield 52 calories.

Types of apricots: Earliest to market and in greatest supply are the California Royals, an orange-to-yellow fruit with a light blush. These are followed by Tiltons, Moorparks, and Washington Perfections. All varieties of apricots are suitable for eating fresh, freezing, or canning.

How apricots are processed: Fresh apricots are available from May to August. Unfortunately, tree-ripened apricots are only available in or near the growing areas or from your own backyard tree. Because they are delicate and highly perishable, apricots are usually picked for shipping when mature but still firm so they will reach the market in good condition.

Since fresh apricots have a short summer season, the other forms in which apricots are marketed are important in bringing the flavor of this fruit into meals all during the year. Canned whole apricots, usually unpeeled, and apricot halves packed in syrup are available. These are graded according to United States standards.

Apricot-Stuffed Chops

These make a man-sized meal—

> 6 to 8 double-rib pork chops
> 1 12-ounce can vacuum-packed corn with peppers
> ⅓ cup fine dry bread crumbs
> ¼ cup chopped onion
> ½ teaspoon salt
> ½ teaspoon dried thyme leaves, crushed
> Dash ground sage
>
> • • •
>
> 1 30-ounce can whole apricots
> 1 tablespoon bottled steak sauce
> 1 teaspoon salt
> 1 teaspoon whole cloves

Cut pocket in each chop, cutting from fat side *almost* to bone edge. Season with salt and pepper. Combine corn, crumbs, onion, the ½ teaspoon salt, thyme, and sage. Spoon the stuffing lightly into chops.

Arrange chops in single layer in 13x9x2-inch baking dish. Cover tightly with foil. Bake at 350° for 30 minutes.

Meanwhile drain syrup from apricots into medium saucepan; stir in steak sauce and the 1 teaspoon salt. Boil uncovered until reduced to ½ cup. Stud apricots with cloves.

Uncover chops (do not turn) and bake 45 minutes longer. Add apricots to baking dish. Brush chops and apricots with glaze. Bake, uncovered, 25 minutes more. Garnish with parsley, if desired. Makes 6 to 8 servings.

Perk up pork chops

Colorful clove-studded, whole apricots and corn stuffing add a mouth-watering touch to Apricot Stuffed Chops.

Unpeeled dried apricot halves, graded according to size, are also available. These fruits have a large percentage of the moisture removed and are treated with sulfur dioxide to aid in color retention. A pretenderization process introduced in recent years has shortened the time necessary for rehydration and stewing of dried apricots. The uncooked dried apricots are nutritious and delicious for out-of-hand eating, and are sometimes called a "fruit candy."

Apricot nectar, the fairly thick and very flavorful pressed juice of ripe apricots, is canned for use as a beverage. Shoppers will also find spiced whole apricots-in-syrup which are canned in jars and used as an accompaniment to meat and poultry.

Apricots are also available in preserves, jam, and pie filling.

How to select: A golden yellow color, plumpness, and firmness are indications of good quality in apricots. Since fresh apricots are an extremely delicate fruit, avoid buying those that are soft to the touch, have dark spots, or a wilted or shriveled look about them.

At peak ripeness apricots are richest in distinctive apricot flavor. Immature or underripe fruits have little of the desired apricot flavor or color.

There are 8 to 12 fresh apricots in a pound. One pound of dried apricots will give 5 cups of cooked apricots.

How to store: Eating-ripe fresh apricots should be refrigerated loosely covered or in a perforated plastic bag to allow the fruit to "breathe." Less ripe apricots should be ripened at room temperature for a day or two, then refrigerated.

Both canned and dried apricots should be stored in a cool, dry place.

How to prepare: Fresh apricots should be washed, then the skin stripped off with a paring knife. If the fruit is still firm, it may be dipped into boiling water for about 30 seconds, then washed with cold water to make peeling easier. Fresh apricots can also be used unpeeled.

Canned apricots, apricot nectar, spiced apricots, apricot preserves, jam, and pie filling can be used directly from the can.

To cook dried apricots, rinse and cover with water 1 inch above fruit in saucepan. Bring water to boiling over medium heat. Reduce heat, cover, and simmer for 20 to 25 minutes, or until tender. If desired, sweeten by adding 3 to 4 tablespoons of sugar per cup of uncooked fruit during the last 5 minutes of cooking.

Fresh Apricot Pie

Prepare pastry for 2-crust 9-inch pie (See *Pastry*) and line pie plate with pastry; fill with 3 cups fresh apricot halves. Combine 1 cup sugar, 3 tablespoons all-purpose flour, and ¼ teaspoon ground nutmeg; sprinkle over apricots in pastry shell.

Drizzle 1 tablespoon lemon juice over fruit; dot with 1 tablespoon butter. Adjust the top crust, cutting slits for the escape of steam; seal. Bake at 425° about 25 to 30 minutes.

Coconut-Apricot Cake

  6 tablespoons butter or margarine
⅔ cup brown sugar
  1 tablespoon light corn syrup
  1 3½-ounce can (1⅓ cups) flaked
     coconut
  1 17-ounce can apricot halves,
     drained
  1 cup sifted all-purpose flour
¾ cup sugar
1¼ teaspoons baking powder
¼ teaspoon salt
¼ cup shortening
  1 egg
½ cup milk
½ teaspoon vanilla

Melt butter or margarine in an 8x8x2-inch baking pan. Stir in brown sugar, corn syrup, and flaked coconut. Pat evenly on bottom and sides of pan. Arrange apricot halves, cut side up, over coconut in bottom of pan.

Into small mixing bowl sift flour, sugar, baking powder, and salt. Add shortening, egg, milk, and vanilla; blend at low speed on electric mixer, then beat at medium speed 2 minutes. Spread over apricots. Bake at 375° for 45 to 50 minutes. Cool 1 to 2 minutes; turn out on serving plate. Serve warm.

Orange-Apricot Freeze

 2 8-ounce cartons (2 cups) orange-
　　flavored yogurt
 1 17-ounce can apricot halves
½ cup sugar
⅓ cup coarsely chopped pecans

Stir yogurt in carton to blend. Drain apricots; cut up fruit. Combine yogurt, apricots, sugar, and chopped pecans. Line muffin pans with 12 paper bake cups. Spoon yogurt mixture into bake cups. Freeze till firm.

Remove bake cups from frozen salads; let stand at room temperature a few minutes before serving. Makes 12 servings.

Apricot Ladder Loaf

¾ cup warm water (110°)
 1 package hot roll mix
 1 egg
 2 tablespoons butter or margarine,
　　melted
　　• • •
½ cup apricot preserves
⅓ cup butter or margarine,
　　softened
⅓ cup chopped blanched almonds,
　　toasted

In the ¾ cup warm water, soften yeast from the hot roll mix as directed on package; stir in *half* of the roll mix. Beat in the egg and melted butter or margarine. Stir in remaining roll mix. Cover; let rise in warm place till double, about 1 hour.

On lightly floured surface knead about 1 minute. Divide dough in half; cover; let rest for 5 minutes. Roll each half to a 9-inch square. Place on greased baking sheets.

Combine apricot preserves, the softened butter or margarine, and almonds; spread in a 3-inch strip down center of each square of dough. With kitchen shears, snip sides toward center in strips 1 inch wide. Fold side strips over filling, alternating from side to side.

Cover; let rise in warm place till almost double, about 45 minutes. Bake at 375° for 20 minutes or till browned. Cool slightly; drizzle with confectioners' sugar icing. (If desired, leave one loaf unfrosted and freeze to use later.) Makes 2 loaves.

Spice the mid-day coffee break with Apricot Ladder Loaf. The apricot-almond filling makes a something-special bread.

Easy Apricot Soufflé

 2 packages vanilla whipped
　　dessert mix
 1 12-ounce can (1½ cups) apricot
　　nectar, chilled
 1 cup canned apricot pie filling

In a deep narrow bowl thoroughly blend the dessert mix and *1 cup* of the apricot nectar. Whip at highest speed of electric mixer for 1 minute. Add remaining apricot nectar; whip at highest speed 2 minutes longer.

With kitchen shears snip through apricots in apricot pie filling. Fold pie filling into the whipped mixture; smooth top.

Chill till set, about 2 to 3 hours. Unmold on dessert platter; garnish with pressurized whipped cream and additional apricot pie filling. Makes 6 to 8 servings.

Apricot Chiffon Pie

A make-ahead dessert—

  ⅓ cup sugar
  1 envelope unflavored gelatin
    Dash salt
  1 12-ounce can apricot nectar
  3 slightly beaten egg yolks
  1 tablespoon lemon juice
  3 egg whites
  2 tablespoons sugar
  ½ cup whipping cream
    Coconut Crust

In medium saucepan combine ⅓ cup sugar, gelatin, and salt. Stir in apricot nectar and slightly beaten egg yolks. Cook and stir over medium heat till gelatin dissolves and mixture thickens slightly. Remove from heat; add lemon juice; chill, stirring occasionally, till the mixture is partially set.

Beat egg whites to soft peaks; gradually add the 2 tablespoons sugar and beat to stiff peaks. Fold in gelatin mixture. Whip cream till stiff; fold into gelatin mixture. Chill until mixture mounds. Pile in cooled Coconut Crust. Chill 4 to 6 hours before serving. Makes one 9-inch pie.

Coconut Crust: Combine one 3½-ounce can (1⅓ cups) flaked coconut and 2 tablespoons butter or margarine, melted. Press into a 9-inch pie plate. Bake at 325° for 15 minutes or till coconut is lightly browned. Cool.

Although fresh apricots have a limited availability, the other forms make it possible to use this flavorful fruit all year round. Fresh, canned, and dried apricots as well as apricot nectar, jam, pie filling, and preserves all have a variety of uses. Try this "seed of the sun" in salads, pies, sauces, desserts, cakes, punches, fruit compotes, meat dishes, pastries, and glazes. The apricot flavor will add a pleasant touch to all these dishes. (See also *Fruit.*)

Light and delicious

Delicately flavored apricot filling in a crisp coconut crust makes Apricot Chiffon Pie a perfect company dessert.

AQUAVIT, AKVAVIT *(ä' kwuh vēt)*—A Scandinavian liquor which is distilled from grain or potatoes then flavored. A few selected spices are generally accepted as being especially suited to flavoring this liquor. These are caraway seed, aniseed, fennel seed, and bitter orange.

Aquavit is served well chilled but never on ice, swallowed in one gulp, and usually followed by a beer chaser. A Scandinavian smorgasbord is traditionally accompanied by this popular liquor.

The term aquavit was coined during the 13th century in Italy to designate the first liquor distilled from wine and is a modification of the Latin phrase *aqua vitae* or the water of life.

Today, Sweden is generally considered to be the world's foremost producer of aquavit, or "snaps," as it is often called in that country. Sweden's aquavit is distilled from potatoes. Second to Sweden in the production of this liquor is Denmark, where this beverage, usually known as "schnapps," is looked on as the national drink. Schnapps is generally a colorless, nonsweetened beverage.

Aquavit is usually served as an apéritif or at the very beginning of a meal. (See also *Wines and Spirits*.)

ARMAGNAC—A fine French brandy from the Gers region. One distinction is the aging in oak casks. (See *Brandy, Wines and Spirits* for additional information.)

ARMORICAINE *(armuhri' kan)*—The Brittany-style preparation of seafood, especially lobster. The preferred spelling is Americaine. (See *Americaine*.)

AROMA—An agreeable odor or fragrance. The word aroma is used in preference to odor or smell in describing the delectable and detectable fragrance of a food.

The senses of taste and smell are very closely related, therefore the aroma of a food greatly influences our enjoyment of it. People instinctively think that if a food has a pleasant aroma, it will also have a pleasant taste. While generally true, exceptions can be quickly demonstrated by biting into a whole clove or by tasting undiluted vanilla extract.

ARRACK, ARAK, ARRAK *(ar' uhk)*—A very strong, fiery liquor that is the native spirit of a number of countries in the Middle East and the Orient. Its base varies in the different countries, but the potency of the liquor is universal.

In the East Indies arrack is distilled from fermented palm sap, molasses, or rice. In the Middle East it is derived from dates. In Indonesia the name is given to a pungent, aromatic type of rum. The flavor of almost any type of arrack is enjoyed most by natives of the country where it's made, but little by outsiders. (See also *Wines and Spirits*.)

ARROWROOT—An easily digestible starch obtained from a tropical American plant of the same name. The rootstalks of the arrowroot plant are peeled, washed, and pulped to produce a white fluid. This fluid is then dried and milled to yield the arrowroot powder used as a thickener.

Arrowroot has no distinct flavor and is an excellent thickener. It is particularly suited for thickening delicately flavored puddings, soups, gravies, and sauces. Foods thickened with arrowroot have a clear, lustrous appearance.

When thickening sauces or puddings, arrowroot is mixed with a cold liquid then cooked, with a minimum of stirring, until the sauce is clear. Sauces thickened with arrowroot reach their maximum thickness at 158° to 176° and heating past this temperature causes marked thinning. To use as a thickener in home cooking, substitute 1½ teaspoons arrowroot powder for every tablespoon of flour.

Although our grandmothers used arrowroot to thicken their famous blancmange, it is rarely used in modern American home-cooking. Arrowroot now is used mainly as a commercial thickening agent for various puddings and other desserts.

ARROZ *(ä rôth')*—The Spanish name for rice. It is found in the title of some popular Spanish-style recipes.

ARROZ CON POLLO *(ä rôth' kôn pô' lyô)*—A Spanish and Mexican dish made of rice, chicken, tomatoes, green pepper, saffron, and other seasonings.

ARTICHOKE *(är' ti chōk')*—A green, thick-leaved vegetable of the sunflower family. A relative of the thistle, the delicately flavored globe or French artichoke is considered a sophisticated vegetable despite its family background.

The globe artichoke was first grown near Naples, Italy, in the middle of the fifteenth century. Gradually plantings spread to other parts of Europe. Reports vary as to when the vegetable was first introduced in the United States. Plantings were made in Louisiana by the French settlers and in the mid-coastal regions of California by the Spaniards around the beginning of the nineteenth century. Artichokes were also cultivated in Florida by early settlers.

How artichokes are grown: Globe artichokes require a cool climate with protection from excessive sunlight and freezing temperatures. Excessive dust is also harmful to the artichoke buds which must "breathe." Thus, the cool, foggy climate of the central California coast and the Mediterranean area are ideal for growing artichokes. California produces most of the artichokes consumed in the United States.

An intriguing vegetable served whole is the globe artichoke. Trim to prepare the casing (left), heart (lower center), or bottom (right) and combine with other foods for gourmet eating.

To prepare whole artichokes, cut off 1 inch from top. Chop stem close to base; remove loose leaves. Snip off sharp leaf tips.

To prepare artichoke bottoms, remove stem and lower leaves. Cut top leaves ½ inch above base. Scoop out choke; shape into cup.

To eat whole artichoke, pull off leaf and dip base into dipping sauce. Draw leaf between teeth, eating only the tender base.

Nutritional value: Globe artichokes do not have great nutritive value, but they contain small amounts of many vitamins and minerals that are important insofar as they supplement other foods in the diet. They are low in calories—44 calories in the base and soft ends of the leaves per 100 grams of cooked artichoke. They are, however, often accompanied with a rich, flavorful sauce.

Types and structure: The globe or French artichoke, the most common type, is grown for its edible floral head. The Jerusalem or Chinese artichoke, a tuberous root of a different member of the sunflower family, resembles the globe or French variety only in flavor.

The globe artichoke is actually the unopened flower bud from the artichoke plant. The edible part is the fleshy base of the leaves (bracts) and the heart inside the leaves. The heart resembles a tiny whole artichoke. The fuzzy core called the choke must be removed (it's prickly if eaten) before the heart can be enjoyed. In very small artichokes, the choke has not developed to a hard core so it may be eaten with the rest of the artichoke.

How to select: Fresh whole globe artichokes are most plentiful during their peak months—August through May—though a limited quantity is available throughout the year. Look for a heavy, compact, globular head which yields slightly to pressure. The leaf scales should be fleshy, cling tightly, and have a healthy green color.

Brown tipped leaves do not necessarily mean inferior quality as artichokes are sensitive and easily bruised or discolored by frost. However, if the leaves are both discolored *and* spread apart, this is an indication that the artichoke is not at its best eating quality.

Likewise, the quality of an artichoke is not determined by its size. The size is governed only by the artichoke's position on the plant. The largest grow near the top of the plant and these may be split in half after cooking for two servings. The smallest artichokes are picked near the base and are most often processed and sold as frozen or canned hearts. Medium-sized artichokes, appropriately found near the center of the plant, and small buds are used most often for individual servings.

How to store: Wrap unwashed artichokes in a plastic bag or in clear plastic wrap and refrigerate. They should keep satisfactorily for several days. At cool temperatures artichokes may be sprinkled lightly with water to minimize wilting and drying. At warm temperatures, sprinkling may cause decay where the water settles between the leaves.

How to use: Due to the manner in which whole artichokes must be eaten, they are often served as an appetizer or as a separate course during the meal. Or, they may be stuffed with meat, fish, poultry, or fresh vegetables, and served either hot or chilled as a main dish salad.

To eat a whole artichoke pull off the leaves or petals one by one and dip the base (light colored end) into melted butter, mayonnaise, Hollandaise, or other seasoned sauce. Eat only the tender part of the leaf by drawing it between the teeth; discard the remaining less-tender end. Continue pulling off the leaves until the fuzzy center or "choke" appears. Remove the choke

Gourmet fare

Elegant Sauterne Sauce caps Lamb-Stuffed Artichokes for a sophisticated entrée. Garnish with lemon slice twist, if desired.

with a knife and fork and discard. Cut the remaining heart into bite-sized pieces with a fork; dip into the sauce and eat.

When the artichoke is stuffed, as in Lamb-Stuffed Artichokes, eat the filling along with the tender ends of the leaves. Once the stuffing has been enjoyed, the heart—considered the most prized part of the artichoke—can be cut, dipped in additional sauce, and savored. Medium-size artichokes are best for stuffing.

Lamb-Stuffed Artichokes

> 4 whole fresh artichokes
> 1 pound ground lamb
> ¾ cup chopped onion
> 2 tablespoons salad oil
> ½ cup fine dry bread crumbs
> ¼ cup snipped parsley
> 2 beaten eggs
> ¼ teaspoon ground nutmeg
> ¼ teaspoon pepper
> Sauterne Sauce

To stuff, remove center leaves and scoop out choke from cooked artichoke. Spoon meat filling into center before baking.

Wash artichokes; cut off stem close to base. Cook in boiling, salted water 25 to 30 minutes or till stalk can be pierced easily and leaf pulled out readily. Drain upside down. Cut off top third of leaves with kitchen shears; remove center leaves and chokes.

Brown lamb and onion in hot oil; drain. Add crumbs, next 4 ingredients, and ½ teaspoon salt; mix well. Spread artichoke leaves slightly; fill centers with meat mixture. Place in 9x9x2-inch baking dish. Pour hot water around artichokes, 1 inch deep. Bake, uncovered, at 375° for 35 minutes.

Serve with *Sauterne Sauce:* Combine ¼ cup sauterne with 1 tablespoon instant minced onion; let stand 10 minutes. Add ¾ cup mayonnaise, 2 tablespoons snipped parsley, and 1 tablespoon lemon juice; mix well. Cook and stir till hot; *do not boil.* Serves 4.

How to prepare: Wash artichokes thoroughly, then cut stem to a one-inch length. Remove any loose outer leaves. Cut off about one inch from top. Snip sharp leaf tips off with scissors to remove thorny tips. Brush the cut edges with lemon juice to prevent darkening. If artichokes are to be stuffed, spread open by placing upside down on a table or board and pressing down firmly. This makes it easier to remove the center leaves and choke before stuffing the vegetable.

Artichokes not only darken when exposed to air, but also when in contact with aluminum, tin, or steel. Therefore, stainless steel, enamelware, pottery, or glass should be used for cooking. As a further precaution to avoid darkening, a small amount of lemon juice or vinegar may be added to the water when cooking.

To boil artichokes, drop the prepared artichokes into a large kettle of boiling, salted water. Cover; simmer for 20 to 30 minutes or till stem is tender and a leaf can be pulled easily from the base. Drain; stuff or serve cold with a sauce.

To steam artichokes, place them in 1 inch of boiling water or on a trivet 1 to 2 inches above boiling water. Sprinkle with salt. Cover and cook as for boiled artichokes but allow 10 to 25 minutes more cooking time, depending upon the size.

Artichoke casings are sometimes served hot, stuffed with meat or creamed vegetables. To prepare casings, slice off the top third of the artichoke. Using a melon-ball cutter or a sharp-edged spoon, scoop out the fuzzy choke and enough additional center leaves to make a generous hollow. Remove all coarse outer leaves and stem. Cook casings covered in a small amount of boiling, salted water, the same as for whole artichokes. When tender, turn upside down to drain. If desired, artichokes may first be cooked whole and then trimmed to make the casings.

Artichoke bottoms, also, may be served hot and filled with creamed foods. Or, marinate cooked bottoms and serve cold as a salad base. Prepare by removing all leaves and the choke from the whole artichoke. (The leaves may be cooked separately, then the edible portion scraped off and used in salad dressings or sauces.) Remove the stem; shape the base into a cup by trimming with a sharp knife. Cook covered in boiling, salted water till bottoms are fork-tender. Drain and serve as desired. To eliminate pre-preparation, buy canned or frozen bottoms.

Artichoke hearts also are available frozen or canned. Served hot, they are a flavorful addition to omelets and casseroles. Canned marinated hearts, also on the market, are delectable served cold as a relish or tossed with a crisp salad. (See *Chinese Artichoke, Jerusalem Artichoke, Vegetable, Sauces* for additional information.)

Marinated Artichokes

1 tablespoon sugar
2 tablespoons lemon juice
2 tablespoons salad oil
1/4 teaspoon *each* dried oregano leaves, crushed, and dried tarragon leaves, crushed
Dash garlic salt
1 15-ounce can artichoke hearts, drained

Combine all ingredients and 2 tablespoons water in a bowl. Cover; chill thoroughly. Drain; sprinkle chilled hearts with paprika, if desired. Serve with cocktail picks. Makes 2 cups.

Artichoke Heart Salad

In saucepan heat to boiling 1/2 cup olive *or* salad oil; 1/3 cup vinegar; 4 thin slices onion; 1 tablespoon sugar; 2 tablespoons water; 1 clove garlic, crushed; 1/2 teaspoon salt; 1/4 teaspoon celery seed; and dash pepper. Add one 9-ounce package frozen artichoke hearts; cook till tender, about 3 to 5 minutes. Cool.

Stir in one 4-ounce can pimientos, chopped, and one 2-ounce can anchovy fillets, drained and diced. Chill thoroughly.

Drain artichoke mixture, reserving dressing. Add artichoke mixture to 2 cups *each* torn lettuce, torn romaine, and torn fresh spinach. Toss with enough reserved dressing to coat salad greens. Makes 8 to 10 servings.

Parsley-Chive Dip for Artichokes

Serve this dip with lemon-mayonnaise and melted butter for an assortment of dipping sauces—

Combine 1 cup dairy sour cream, 1 tablespoon chopped chives, 1 tablespoon snipped parsley, 1 teaspoon lemon juice, and several drops bottled hot pepper sauce; blend well. Chill.

Serve as dipping sauce for whole fresh artichokes, cooked and drained. Makes 1 cup.

Artichoke Velvet

2 9-ounce packages frozen artichoke hearts
1 pint fresh mushrooms, sliced
2 tablespoons butter
1 envelope chicken gravy mix
Dash dried ground thyme
Dash dried ground marjoram
4 ounces Swiss cheese, diced (1 cup)
1 tablespoon dry white wine

Cook artichokes according to package directions; drain. Cook mushrooms in butter till tender. Combine artichokes and mushrooms in 1-quart casserole. Prepare gravy mix following package directions. Remove from heat; add thyme, marjoram, and cheese. Stir till cheese melts. Stir in wine; pour mixture over vegetables. Bake, covered, at 350° for 30 minutes. Makes 6 to 8 servings.

Filled Artichoke Casings

> 4 or 5 whole fresh artichokes
> 1/4 cup butter or margarine, melted
> 3 tablespoons all-purpose flour
> 1 cup light cream
> 1 cup chicken broth
> 1 teaspoon salt
> 1/2 teaspoon dried tarragon leaves,
>   crushed
> 2 cups diced cooked chicken
> 2 tablespoons dry sherry

With sharp knife, cut off stems of artichokes. Slice off top third of each. Using a melon-ball cutter or sharp-edged spoon, scoop out fuzzy choke and enough additional center leaves to make a generous hollow. Remove all coarse outer leaves. Set casings upright in small amount of boiling, salted water. Cover; simmer 25 to 30 minutes or till stalk can be pierced easily and leaf pulls out readily. Remove and turn upside down to drain.

In saucepan blend butter with flour; stir in cream and chicken broth. Cook over medium heat, stirring constantly, till mixture thickens and bubbles. Stir in salt, tarragon, and diced chicken. Heat through. Just before serving, stir in sherry. Spoon creamed chicken mixture into hot cooked casings. Makes 4 or 5 servings.

Crab-Artichoke Bake

> 2 7 1/2-ounce cans crab meat, drained,
>   flaked, and cartilage removed
> 4 ounces process Swiss cheese,
>   cubed (1 cup)
> 1/3 cup chopped green pepper
> 1/4 cup finely chopped onion
> 1 teaspoon salt
> 1/2 cup mayonnaise
> 2 teaspoons lemon juice
> 5 whole fresh artichokes, cooked
>   and drained

Toss together crab, cheese, green pepper, onion, and salt. Blend mayonnaise with lemon juice. Toss with crab mixture. Remove small center leaves of artichokes, leaving a cup. Remove chokes. Fill artichokes with crab salad. Place in 12x7 1/2x2-inch baking dish. Pour hot water around them 1/4 inch deep. Cover and bake at 375° for 35 minutes. Makes 5 servings.

ARTIFICIAL—Used to describe ingredients found in foods which have been chemically synthesized to resemble natural food substances. Artificial sweeteners, flavorings, and colorings are found on many food labels in the market.

ASCORBIC ACID *(ā skôr' bik, uh skôr')*— The chemical name for vitamin C. The functions of ascorbic acid in the body include making the cementing substance between the cells of the body, increasing the strength of the blood vessel walls, hastening the healing of injuries, and helping the body resist infection.

The absence of this vitamin in the diet causes bleeding gums, loosening of teeth, soreness in the joints, weight loss, and fatigue. In extreme cases, the vitamin deficiency condition is called scurvy.

In the mid-eighteenth century, an English doctor discovered that eating oranges and lemons caused a rapid cure of scurvy symptoms. He recommended that the juice of lemons (then called limes) be carried on all British ships to protect the health of the sailors. Thus, British sailors became known as "limeys."

The body does not store large amounts of ascorbic acid. Therefore, it is important that it is included daily in the diet. The best sources of this vitamin include cantaloupe, oranges, grapefruit, lemons, limes, strawberries, tomatoes, green peppers, and green and leafy vegetables such as cabbage.

Ascorbic acid, the least stable of all vitamins, is water-soluble and easily destroyed by heat. Thus, soaking of vegetables in water should be avoided. They should be cooked quickly in the least amount of water possible.

The vitamin is also lost when exposed to air. Consequently, when squeezing fresh fruits, such as oranges, prepare the juice just before serving. If prepared ahead, cover and store in the refrigerator for as short a time as possible.

Ascorbic acid is also used commercially as a color keeper. Small amounts are used to prevent the discoloration of cut fruits and vegetables, such as apples, peaches, pears, and artichokes. *(See Color Keeper, Nutrition* for additional information.)

ASPARAGUS—The edible, green-to-whitish tender shoots of a perennial vegetable of the lily family. The most noticeable characteristic of all asparagus is the apparent absence of leaves. Although leaves are present, they are reduced to small scales on the stalk.

Male asparagus plants are the most prolific and produce slender spears. The female plants can be recognized because they flower and have a seed pod. Female plants produce the largest spears.

This vegetable as known in the United States today is just one of about 150 asparagus species that are edible.

While asparagus is known generally for its food value, some species are grown in greenhouses and flower gardens as ornamental plants. If left uncut, the asparagus plant will grow into a tall, lacy bush, equal in beauty to the most delicate fern.

The name, asparagus, comes from a Greek word meaning "stalk" or "shoot." Asparagus is believed to have originated in the eastern Mediterranean lands and Asia Minor. The plant commonly grows wild over much of that area today and also in Europe, and even in many places in the United States where it has escaped from cultivation. This vegetable thrives along riverbanks, shores of fresh- and saltwater lakes, and sandy seacoasts. Asparagus has been found "wild" in so many places that there has been much argument as to where it actually originated.

The ancient Greeks apparently collected only wild asparagus since they left no directions for cultivating it. As early as 200 B.C., however, Roman gardeners wrote down detailed instructions for the cultivation of this vegetable.

The Romans were the first asparagus "processors"—drying it in season for later use. It was then simply and quickly prepared by boiling the dried shoots. Preparation was considered so simple that the Roman Emperor Augustus is reputed to have said of anything fast: "quicker than you can cook asparagus."

Quick frozen asparagus dates back to the first century when the Feast of Epicurus was a very important celebration in Rome. Fast chariots and runners were dispatched from the Tiber River carrying

According to Chinese philosophy, overcooking ruins vegetables, so the Chinese developed and have become famous for the "stir-fry" or "toss-cook" cooking method. Using this method, the cooking time is watched very closely to obtain vegetables that are still crisp, yet tender and at peak flavor. With green vegetables, cooking is done "to color" and stops when the vegetables are between "bright" and "dark" green, usually closer to "bright." To prove the merit of this cookery method try Asparagus Oriental.

asparagus to the snow line of the Alps where it was kept frozen until the feast was held six months later.

Fresh asparagus held a place in the medical field of the ancients. The vegetable was thought to have many medicinal properties including the prevention of heart trouble and the relief of bee stings.

Englishmen and many North Europeans have been eating fresh asparagus since the days of their first recorded history. The early English developed a fondness for eating it raw as well as cooked.

Undoubtedly some of our earliest settlers brought asparagus roots with them from Europe. Thomas Jefferson cultivated asparagus in his greenhouses at Monticello. Pioneers taking the asparagus plant with them as they traveled west developed colloquial names for it. From these we get "sparrow grass" and "sparagrass." Even today, asparagus is sometimes called "grass" in the vegetable trade.

Since ancient times, asparagus has been considered a luxury item, fit for a king. This vegetable continues to be a favorite at gourmet dinners, and chefs all over the world have used asparagus in creating some of their most famous dishes.

Asparagus Oriental

    1 tablespoon salad oil
    3 cups fresh asparagus in bias-
        cut pieces 1½ inches long
    ½ teaspoon salt
    ½ teaspoon monosodium glutamate
        Dash pepper

Heat salad oil in a large skillet; add the pieces of asparagus. Sprinkle with salt, monosodium glutamate, and pepper. Cover. Lift skillet slightly above high heat and shake it constantly while cooking.

Cook asparagus only till tender, 4 to 5 minutes. Reduce heat to medium, if necessary, during last minute or so of cooking. Don't overcook. Makes 6 servings.

Nutritional value: Fresh asparagus is low in calories (⅔ cup cooked=20 calories), a fair source of vitamin C, and an excellent source of the drug rutin. This drug is important in the body for strengthening the walls of the small blood vessels and thus important in reducing the possibility of hemorrhaging. The water-soluble vitamin C may be lost during cooking.

Imagination is the key when saucing asparagus. Classic Hollandaise over asparagus spears is one suggestion (See *Hollandaise Sauce* for recipe). Top with hard-cooked egg slices.

To cut up fresh asparagus spears, slice several spears at a time with long diagonal strokes, or cut straight across.

Make an asparagus cooker. Place strip of folded aluminum foil across bottom and up sides of pan, extending over edges.

To use an asparagus cooker, lay fresh asparagus spears on rack. Cook in boiling salted water till tender. Lift rack to drain.

Types of asparagus: Green and white asparagus are the two types of asparagus usually available to consumers. Although both types are of the same plant variety, different growing techniques are used to result in the presence or absence of the green pigment, chlorophyll.

Since sunlight is necessary for the production of chlorophyll, green asparagus is grown in a nearly level field where it gets plenty of sunlight. To produce white or bleached asparagus, the plant is cut off at ground level and protected from the sunlight by heaping mounds of dirt around it. The tender, white spears are cut as soon as a tiny tip peeks through the mound.

Although most white asparagus is used for canning, green asparagus is marketed fresh, canned, and frozen.

How to select: Fresh asparagus appears on the market as early as February with the beginning of the California crop. The season continues until late June when the New Jersey crop disappears.

When purchasing either variety choose stalks that look crisp and fresh and have only a couple of inches of light-colored woody base. The tips should be well formed and tightly closed. Wilted, crooked, very thin, or very thick stalks are likely to be tough, woody, or stringy.

Fresh asparagus is sold by the pound or by the bunch. One pound of fresh asparagus makes three or four servings or yields two cups when cut.

Frozen asparagus, spears and cuts, and canned asparagus, whole or cut, may be purchased all year round.

How to store: Fresh asparagus should be stored in a refrigerator—in a tightly sealed container or plastic bag. The stem ends should be kept in moist toweling, or resting in a little water. If the stalks seem limp, cut a thin slice from the ends and stand stalks in cold water briefly before storing. Fresh asparagus is delicate and highly perishable so it should be used soon after purchase.

Frozen asparagus should be kept frozen until used. If frozen asparagus becomes partially thawed, use it promptly. Store canned asparagus in a cool, dry place.

How to prepare: To clean fresh asparagus, wash the stalks thoroughly and scrape off the scales to remove hidden sand. The asparagus may be peeled, if desired. To remove the woody base, break the stalks instead of cutting; they will snap where the tender part starts. The fresh asparagus is now ready to cook.

There are several methods of cooking asparagus. Choose one of the following depending on availability of kitchen utensils and personal preference.

To cook asparagus standing up, fasten asparagus in a bundle, using a band of foil, and stand the stalks upright with the tips extending 1 inch or more above boiling salted water in a tall glass percolator or a deep kettle. If the stalks tend to fall over, prop up the bundle with crumpled foil. Cover and cook for 10 to 15 minutes, or till tender. The tips cook in steam while the stalks cook in boiling water.

Another method of cooking asparagus is in a skillet. Lay the asparagus spears flat in the skillet, add a small amount of boiling salted water and cover with tight-fitting lid. Cook till just tender, about 10 to 15 minutes. To avoid overcooking the tender tips, prop them up out of the water with crushed foil at one side of the pan. The tips will cook in steam while the stalks cook in water.

To use a saucepan for cooking asparagus, cut a strip of aluminum foil to place across bottom and up both sides of saucepan extending over edges. Fold, making strip 4 to 5 inches wide. Lay asparagus on foil in pan. Add small amount of boiling water and salt. Cover with tight-fitting lid and cook till just tender, about 10 to 15 minutes. Remove asparagus from saucepan by lifting ends of foil strip.

If cut-up asparagus is desired, use this method of cooking. Cut stalks in pieces, several at a time. Cook, covered, in small amount of boiling salted water till just tender, about 8 to 10 minutes.

Overcooking makes asparagus watery, limp, and dark, and robs it of flavor.

Cook frozen asparagus according to label directions. Chill canned green or white asparagus thoroughly for salads. Heat canned asparagus according to label directions if to be served hot.

Asparagus Casserole

    2 tablespoons butter or margarine
    2 tablespoons all-purpose flour
    ½ teaspoon salt
      Dash pepper
    2 cups milk
          • • •
    2 pounds fresh asparagus, cut crosswise in 1½-inch pieces (4 cups) and cooked
    4 hard-cooked eggs, sliced
    ¼ cup medium saltine cracker crumbs
    2 tablespoons butter or margarine, melted

Melt 2 tablespoons butter or margarine; blend in flour, salt, and pepper. Add milk all at once. Cook, stirring constantly, till mixture thickens and bubbles. Arrange *half* the cooked asparagus and all the hard-cooked egg slices in bottom of 8x8x2-inch baking dish.

Add *half* the white sauce. Top with remaining asparagus and sauce. Toss crumbs with melted butter or margarine; sprinkle over casserole. Bake at 350° for 30 to 35 minutes, or till heated through. Makes 6 servings.

Asparagus in Blankets

    1 10-ounce package frozen asparagus spears
    2 cups packaged biscuit mix
    2 tablespoons butter, melted
    1 2½-ounce jar dried beef
      Cheese Sauce

Cook asparagus in boiling salted water according to package directions. Prepare biscuit mix according to package directions for rolled biscuits. Divide dough in half; roll in two 12-inch circles. Brush dough with butter. Cut each circle into 6 wedges.

Divide asparagus and dried beef into 12 equal portions and place crosswise on wide end of wedges; roll. Press to seal tip. Bake on greased baking sheet at 450° for 10 minutes or till lightly browned.

Serve with *Cheese Sauce:* Mix one 10¾-ounce can condensed Cheddar cheese soup and ¼ teaspoon dried marjoram leaves, crushed; heat, but do not boil. Serve hot. Serves 6.

Chilled Asparagus Soup

    1 10-ounce package frozen cut
        asparagus
    2 cups milk
    1 teaspoon instant minced onion
    1 teaspoon salt
      Dash pepper
    ½ cup light cream
      Dairy sour cream

Cook asparagus according to package directions; drain well. Combine asparagus, *1 cup* of the milk, onion, salt, and pepper in a blender container. Blend till smooth, about 10 seconds. Add remaining milk; blend 5 seconds. Add light cream; blend 5 seconds.

Chill 3 to 4 hours. Top servings with dollops of sour cream. Makes 4 to 6 servings.

Asparagus Toss

    1 pound fresh asparagus, cut
        in 2-inch pieces (2 cups)
    1 small head lettuce, torn in
        bite-size pieces (4 cups)
    1 cup sliced celery
    ¼ cup sliced green onion
        and tops
    ½ cup salad oil
    2 tablespoons white wine vinegar
    2 tablespoons lemon juice
    ¼ cup finely chopped cooked
        beets
    1 hard-cooked egg, finely chopped
    1 tablespoon snipped parsley
    1 teaspoon paprika
    1 teaspoon sugar
    1 teaspoon salt
    ½ teaspoon dry mustard
    4 drops bottled hot pepper sauce

Cook asparagus till just tender; drain. Chill. Combine with lettuce, celery, and onion.

For dressing*, combine salad oil, vinegar, lemon juice, beets, egg, parsley, paprika, sugar, salt, dry mustard, and hot pepper sauce in screw-top jar; cover and shake well. Pour dressing over salad; toss lightly till well coated. Makes 6 to 8 servings.

*If desired, use one envelope French salad dressing mix and omit the last 5 ingredients listed above.

Asparagus Amandine

Cook 2 pounds fresh asparagus spears *or* two 10-ounce packages frozen asparagus spears in boiling salted water till tender; drain well. In small skillet cook ¼ cup slivered almonds in ¼ cup butter over low heat till golden brown, about 5 to 7 minutes, stirring constantly. Remove from heat; add ½ teaspoon salt and 1 tablespoon lemon juice and pour over asparagus. Makes 6 servings.

Asparagus-Tomato Salad

    2 pounds fresh asparagus spears,
        cooked and drained
    ⅓ cup mayonnaise
    1¼ teaspoons lemon juice
    1 medium tomato, peeled and
        diced

Keep asparagus hot. In small saucepan combine mayonnaise, lemon juice, ¼ teaspoon salt, and ⅛ teaspoon pepper. Stir over low heat till heated through. Stir in tomato; heat through. Serve over asparagus. Serves 6.

Molded Asparagus Salad

    1 envelope (1 tablespoon)
        unflavored gelatin
    1 10½-ounce can condensed cream
        of asparagus soup
    1 tablespoon lemon juice
    ¼ teaspoon salt
    1 8-ounce carton (1 cup) cream-
        style cottage cheese
    ½ cup dairy sour cream
                • • •
    1 10½-ounce can asparagus spears,
        drained and cut
    ½ cup chopped celery
    2 tablespoons chopped canned
        pimiento

In saucepan soften gelatin in ¼ cup cold water. Stir over low heat till gelatin is dissolved. Blend soup, lemon juice, and salt into gelatin; beat in cottage cheese and sour cream. Chill gelatin mixture till partially set, then fold in remaining ingredients. Pour into 4½-cup mold. Chill till firm. Makes 5 or 6 servings.

Impress guests with Tomato-Celery Aspic filled with Swedish Pickled Shrimp, a favorite seafood, or a well-seasoned chicken salad. (See *Scandinavian Cookery* for shrimp recipe.)

Perhaps the most popular way of serving asparagus is piping hot with either melted butter or hollandaise sauce. Imagination, however, is the key to uses for this vegetable. Dip it in melted butter for an appetizer. Combine it with cooked meat and sauce for a special casserole. Add a gourmet touch to the meal by serving an asparagus soufflé.

Asparagus can be served plain or fancy. Sauce it with a variety of butter and cream sauces. Sprinkle it with Parmesan cheese and grill. Serve it creamed on toast. Cut it into pieces and add to a vegetable salad. Coat it with batter and fry. Mold it in gelatin for a salad. Wrap it in meat and pastry and bake. Garnish scrambled or poached eggs, fish, and poultry with asparagus. Make asparagus cream soup from the coarser part of the stalk. Use the leftovers, if there are any, for an omelet filling.

Asparagus has been popular since ancient times and at present is the fifth most popular vegetable in the United States. Although fresh asparagus has a limited availability, frozen and canned asparagus are available all year round. Whether it is served hot, warm, or cold, asparagus is "fit for a king" and everyone else. (See also *Vegetable*.)

ASPIC—A cold food coated with or molded in a jelly. Originally, the jelly was made of beef, veal, chicken, or fish stock which gelled when cooled because of natural gelatin. Today, however, gelatin is often added to firm the gel.

Aspics are used for making molds in which various meats, poultry, seafoods, or vegetables are encased. Foods cooked and thoroughly chilled can be glazed with crystal-clear aspic jelly. To use an aspic

Thinly sliced hard-cooked eggs encircle the Sunshine Aspic mold. Top servings with mayonnaise or salad dressing.

for garnishing, the jelly can either be chopped or cut into various shapes and used for decorative purposes.

In American kitchens the term aspic is often applied to any highly seasoned, colorful, molded gel. These aspics may be either creamy or crystal-clear.

Tomato-Celery Aspic

    4 cups tomato juice
    ⅓ cup chopped onion
    ¼ cup snipped celery leaves
    2 tablespoons brown sugar
    1 teaspoon salt
    2 small bay leaves
    4 whole cloves
    2 envelopes unflavored gelatin
    3 tablespoons lemon juice
    1 cup finely chopped celery

Mix *2 cups* tomato juice with next six ingredients. Simmer uncovered 5 minutes. Strain.

Meanwhile soften gelatin in *1 cup* of remaining cold tomato juice; dissolve in hot mixture. Add remaining tomato juice and the lemon juice. Chill till partially set.

Add celery. Pour into a 5½-cup ring mold. Chill till firm. Makes 8 to 10 servings.

Sunshine Aspic

An elegant buffet or luncheon salad—

    3 cups tomato juice
    1 bay leaf
    ½ teaspoon celery salt
    ½ teaspoon onion salt
    2 3-ounce packages lemon-
       flavored gelatin
    ¾ cup water
    ¼ cup vinegar
         • • •
    3 hard-cooked eggs, shelled
       and sliced

In a small saucepan heat *2 cups* of the tomato juice, the bay leaf, celery salt, and onion salt to boiling. Add gelatin, stirring till dissolved. Remove and discard bay leaf. Add the remaining 1 cup tomato juice, the water, and vinegar. Chill till partially set.

Pour partially set gelatin mixture into 6½-cup ring mold. Carefully push egg slices into gelatin close to outer edge of mold. Chill till firm. Unmold onto serving plate; serve with mayonnaise or salad dressing, if desired. Makes 8 to 10 servings.

Creamy Aspic

A salad that can be made the night before and unmolded at the last minute—

    1 envelope (1 tablespoon)
       unflavored gelatin
    1 12-ounce can vegetable-juice
       cocktail
         • • •
    1 3-ounce package cream cheese,
       softened
    1 teaspoon lemon juice
    ½ teaspoon Worcestershire sauce
    ¼ teaspoon onion juice

In a saucepan soften gelatin in *half* of the vegetable-juice cocktail. Stir over low heat till gelatin is dissolved. Remove from heat; slowly beat into cream cheese with rotary beater. Stir in remaining cocktail, lemon juice, Worcestershire sauce, and onion juice.

Pour into 3½-cup mold. Chill till firm. Unmold on crisp greens. Makes 4 servings.

A crystal-clear, shimmering aspic is an impressive sight when served as a relish. When molded and filled with small pieces of meat, fish, poultry, fruit, or vegetables, an aspic becomes an elegant main dish for a supper, luncheon, or informal buffet. (See also *Salads.*)

ATHOL BROSE *(ath' ôl brōz)*—A traditional Scottish beverage served as a nightcap. Athol brose is made of strained oatmeal water, honey, and whiskey. (See also *Wines and Spirits.*)

AUBERGINE *(ō' bēr zhuhn')*—The French name for eggplant. (See *Eggplant.*)

AU BEURRE *(ō bûr')*—A French menu phrase meaning "with butter." The phrase *au beurre noir* means "with brown butter."

AU GRATIN *(ōgrä'uhn, ōgrat'uhn)*—French phrase literally meaning "with the burnt part." *Au gratin* frequently misused to describe any cooked dish which has cheese as an ingredient, designates a cooking process performed in a hot oven or under the broiler to produce dishes with a crisp, golden-brown crust. This crust is usually achieved by topping the food with fresh or toasted bread crumbs or grated cheese and melted butter. *Au gratin* also applies to dishes that form a crust without any topping being added.

Shredded au Gratin Potatoes

  6 medium potatoes
  1 teaspoon salt
  ¼ teaspoon pepper
   Onion salt
      • • •
  4 ounces sharp process American
    cheese, shredded (1 cup)
  1 cup milk

Cook unpeeled potatoes in water till almost tender. Cool, peel, and shred to make about 4 cups. Place in greased 10x6x1½-inch baking dish. Sprinkle with salt and pepper; sprinkle liberally with onion salt. Top with cheese; pour milk over. Bake at 350° for 30 minutes or till browned. Makes 5 or 6 servings.

Pears au Gratin

  5 ripe pears (2 pounds), peeled,
    cored, and cut in ½-inch
    slices
  ¼ cup apricot preserves
  ¼ cup dry white wine
  ½ cup dry macaroon crumbs
  3 tablespoons butter or margarine

Overlap pear slices in layers in buttered 10x6x1½-inch baking dish. Heat preserves and put through sieve. Add wine to sieved preserves and pour over pears.

Sprinkle with macaroon crumbs and dot with butter or margarine. Bake at 400° for 20 to 25 minutes or till pears are done and crumbs are browned. Serve warm. Makes 4 servings.

Ham and Potatoes au Gratin

  1 12-ounce can chopped ham
  1 package au gratin potato mix
  1 3-ounce can chopped mushrooms,
    drained
  1 teaspoon Worcestershire sauce

Cut meat in 8 slices and place in 10x6x1½-inch baking dish. Top with potato slices from mix. Sprinkle mushrooms over potatoes along with cheese-sauce mix from potato mix.

Continue as directed on package but add Worchestershire sauce to the butter and boiling water called for. Cover and bake at 400° for 40 minutes. Makes 4 servings.

AU JUS *(ō zhōs', ō jōs')*—French menu phrase describing the serving of roast meat plain with its natural juices.

To prepare *au jus* to serve with roast meat, remove the roast from the pan. Skim off the excess fat from the meat juices. Add a little water to the meat juices in the pan. Simmer for about 3 minutes, stirring to remove crusty meat bits. Strain. Serve hot. (See also *Gravy.*)

AU LAIT *(ō lā')*—The French phrase for "with milk," used to describe a food served with milk or cooked in milk. *Café au Lait* is a mixture of coffee and warm milk, usually in equal proportions.

Café au Lait Cheesecake

  ¾ cup sugar
  2 envelopes (2 tablespoons)
      unflavored gelatin
  ¼ teaspoon salt
  2 beaten egg yolks
  1 cup milk
  2 tablespoons instant
      coffee powder
  3 cups cream–style cottage
      cheese
  1 teaspoon vanilla
          •   •   •
  2 egg whites
  ¼ cup sugar
  1 cup whipping cream
          •   •   •
  2 tablespoons butter or margarine
  ½ cup graham cracker crumbs
      (7 crackers)
  1 tablespoon sugar

In saucepan combine the ¾ cup sugar, gelatin, and salt; stir in egg yolks and milk. Cook and stir over low heat till gelatin dissolves. Blend in coffee powder; cool.

Sieve cottage cheese by pushing through a strainer; stir into gelatin mixture along with vanilla. Chill, stirring occasionally, till mixture mounds when spooned. (Mixture will not be smooth due to texture of the cottage cheese.)

Meanwhile beat egg whites to soft peaks; gradually add the ¼ cup sugar, beating to stiff peaks. Whip cream and fold into gelatin mixture; then fold in egg whites. Pour into 8- or 9-inch springform pan.

Melt butter or margarine; add graham cracker crumbs and 1 tablespoon sugar. Sprinkle over cheesecake. Chill 3 to 4 hours; remove sides of springform pan. Serves about 10.

AU NATUREL (*ō nad uh rel′*)—The French menu phrase used to describe food served plain and unsauced or raw.

Luscious Cheesecake

←The coffee-and-cream flavor of Café au Lait Cheesecake makes this cheesecake special, and a truly elegant dessert.

To give the cheesecake a smoother texture, sieve the cottage cheese by pushing it through a large strainer.

Before adding the egg whites and whipped cream, chill the gelatin-cottage cheese mixture until it mounds when spooned.

To make a design on top, sprinkle crumbs around heavy paper pattern centered on cake. Carefully remove pattern.

AUSLESE (*ous' lā zuh*)—A German wine term used to describe wines made from the very best and ripest grapes, specially selected and picked bunch by bunch. (See also *Wines and Spirits*.)

AVGOLEMONO (*äv' gō lem' uh nō*)—A traditional Greek sauce of egg, lemon, and chicken broth. It is served with chicken, fish, or vegetables. Also an ingredient in soups and stews, it acts as a delicate thickener and adds a pleasing golden color as well. (See also *Sauces*.)

AVOCADO—A semitropical, tree-grown fruit, often pear-shaped, with a rich, distinctive flavor. Avocado trees, members of the laurel family, grow in California, Florida, Mexico, Middle and South America, Cuba, Israel, South Africa, and Hawaii.

The ancient peoples of tropical America cultivated the avocado and made it a staple in their diet. The Mayas of Mexico were enjoying the fruit as early as 300 B.C. Ancient Aztecs called it *ahuacatl*. Later avocados were grown in Peru and the West Indies. In fact, George Washington sampled them during a trip to the Barbados in 1751. Mexico was the source of the avocados brought to California for cultivation. Today California leads the world in commercial production.

Nutritional value: The flesh of the avocado contains no starch and only a little sugar. Its fruit-oil content is a source of food energy. Depending on size, half a medium avocado supplies 140 to 165 calories. Several vitamins are present including vitamins A, E, and the B group. Many minerals, particularly iron, are present too.

Names and varieties: The fruit of the avocado tree has had many colorful names. Alligator pear is one and this probably came about because certain pear-shaped varieties have a thick, pebbly skin not unlike alligator hide. Sailors called them midshipman's butter because of their buttery texture. In West Africa avocados are known as custard apples.

There is considerable variation in the shape of avocados found at the produce counter. Some are round, some pear-shaped with long necks, and some are egg-shaped. Regardless of the color or texture of the skin or the shape, the flesh of all these fruits is the same. It is a greenish-yellow with a contrasting bright green next to the skin. It has a velvety, buttery texture and a nutlike flavor.

There is no season for avocados. The winter and summer varieties overlap in arriving on the market. The most familiar winter avocado is green with a smoother skin. The pebbled dark-skinned fruit is the leading summer variety. Its shades range from a deep green to purple to black.

How to select: Avocados are ready to eat only when they have lost their firm feel. Although picked at maturity, the fruit never becomes soft on the tree. Avocados are tender and easily bruised in spite of being shipped while firm. Plan ahead and buy avocados several days before they are to be served. Few are marketed at just the stage of eating ripeness. Left at room temperature for three or four days, they come to perfect softness.

After cutting avocado lengthwise, rotate halves to separate. Strike seed with the sharp edge of knife; twist and lift seed out.

If peeled or cut avocado is not to be used at once, brush with lemon or lime juice to prevent the fruit from turning dark.

To test for ripeness, cup the avocado in the palm of the hand or between both palms. If it yields to gentle pressure, it is ready to eat. Never pinch. This bruises the fruit causing discolored spots. Choose avocados that appear sound and plump and show no signs of withering.

Commercial fast-freezing methods are making possible frozen avocado products such as dips and sauces.

How to store: Hold avocados at room temperature until they are the right softness to eat. This may require several days. Then, refrigerate until ready to use. Sprinkle lemon or lime juice on unused, cut avocado and wrap in foil or airtight wrap before refrigerating. Replace the seed when storing an unused half shell. Although diced avocado is used occasionally in a frozen salad, home freezer storage is limited to the fruit which has been mashed with a little lemon juice and packed in an airtight container.

How to use: Halved and pitted avocados are ready to eat sprinkled with salt and lime or lemon juice. Peeled shells, as well as those with the skin on, make delicious cups for seafood or fruit salads. Use a melon baller to scoop balls from unpeeled shells. Peeled fruit may be sliced in either direction or cubed as a salad ingredient or garnish. Use mashed avocado in a variety of spreads or dips such as the Mexican favorite, Guacamole.

When peeling an avocado half, use the tip of a knife to loosen the skin. Starting at the stem end, lift or strip skin away. When peeled gently, the lovely green outer flesh is left intact. Brush all cut surfaces with lemon juice or ascorbic acid color keeper to prevent darkening. (See *Fruit, Guacamole* for additional information.)

Avocado Cocktail Spread

> 2 **large ripe avocados, pitted, peeled, and slightly mashed**
> 1 **6½-ounce can tuna, drained**
> 2 **tablespoons lemon juice**
> 2 **teaspoons prepared horseradish**
> ½ **teaspoon salt**
> **Dash bottled hot pepper sauce**

Combine all ingredients; mix well. Cover and chill. Serve with crackers. Makes 2 cups.

Avocado Fruit Freeze

> 1 **large avocado**
> 2 **tablespoons lemon juice**
> 1 **3-ounce package cream cheese, softened**
> ¼ **cup mayonnaise or salad dressing**
> 2 **tablespoons sugar**
> ¼ **teaspoon salt**
> 1 **16-ounce can pears, drained and diced (1½ cups)**
> ¼ **cup well-drained chopped maraschino cherries**
> ½ **cup whipping cream**

Pit, peel, and dice avocado; sprinkle with *1 tablespoon* of the lemon juice. Blend cream cheese, remaining lemon juice, mayonnaise, sugar, and salt. Add avocado, pears, and cherries. Whip cream; fold into fruit mixture. Pour into 3-cup refrigerator tray; freeze till firm, about 6 hours or overnight. Let stand at room temperature 15 minutes before serving. Makes 6 servings.

Avocado-Citrus Salad

    1 8½-ounce can grapefruit
        sections
    2 3-ounce packages orange-
        flavored gelatin
    1 7-ounce bottle ginger ale
    2 avocados, halved, pitted,
        peeled, and sliced crosswise

Drain grapefruit, reserving syrup; add water to syrup to make ¾ cup. Dice grapefruit. Dissolve gelatin in 2 cups boiling water. Add reserved syrup mixture to dissolved gelatin; cool. Add ginger ale, pouring slowly down side of bowl, stirring gently with an up-and-down motion. Chill till partially set. Fold in grapefruit and avocado. Pour into 6½-cup mold. Chill 6 to 8 hours or overnight. Serves 8 to 10.

Orange-Avocado Toss

    ⅓ cup French salad dressing
    ½ teaspoon shredded orange peel
    1 medium avocado halved, pitted,
        and peeled
    1 medium orange, sectioned and
        white membrane removed
    2 cups torn Bibb or Boston
        lettuce
    1 green onion, sliced

Combine French dressing and peel; set aside for one hour. Slice avocado into bottom of salad bowl. Cover completely with the orange sections. Top with lettuce and onion. Cover bowl with clear plastic wrap; chill. At serving time add dressing-peel mixture; toss gently. Serve at once. Makes 2 servings.

Avocado Dressing

    ½ cup mashed ripe avocado
    1 tablespoon lemon juice
    2 teaspoons sugar
    ½ cup whipping cream
    ½ teaspoon grated lemon peel

Blend first 3 ingredients and ¼ teaspoon salt. Whip cream; fold into avocado mixture. Sprinkle with the lemon peel. Chill. Serve within a few hours. Makes about 1½ cups.

Apple-Avocado Ring

    1 3-ounce package strawberry-
        flavored gelatin
    1 16-ounce jar spiced apple rings
    1 3-ounce package lemon-flavored
        gelatin
    1 tablespoon lemon juice
    ½ cup whipping cream
    2 avocados, peeled and mashed
        (1 cup)

Dissolve strawberry-flavored gelatin in 1 cup boiling water. Drain apple rings reserving ¼ cup syrup. Add reserved syrup and ¾ cup cold water to dissolved gelatin. Chill till partially set. Dice apple rings, reserving 3 rings for garnish. Fold apple into partially set gelatin. Pour into 6½ cup mold; chill mixture till *almost* firm.

Dissolve lemon-flavored gelatin in 1 cup boiling water. Add ½ cup cold water and lemon juice. Chill till partially set. Whip cream; fold into partially set gelatin with the mashed avocado. Pour mixture over apple layer. Chill till firm. Unmold; garnish with reserved apple rings. Makes 8 servings.

Crab-Stuffed Avocados

    ½ cup mayonnaise or salad
        dressing
    2 hard-cooked eggs, chopped
    ¼ cup chopped celery
    3 tablespoons chopped pimiento
    1 teaspoon dry mustard
    ¼ teaspoon salt
        Dash Worcestershire sauce
    3 medium avocados
        Lemon juice
    ¾ pound chilled, cooked, shelled
        crab legs (about 1½ pounds in
        shell), cut in short lengths
        Lemon wedges

Combine mayonnaise, chopped hard-cooked eggs, celery, pimiento, dry mustard, salt, and Worcestershire sauce. Refrigerate; chill mixture thoroughly.

Halve avocados lengthwise; carefully twist to remove seed. Brush avocados with lemon juice to retain color. Fill avocado halves with egg mixture and top with crab. Serve with lemon wedges. Makes 6 servings.

Buttery-smooth avocado is a tempting partner for shrimp and
one of New Orleans' favorite sauces. Chilled vegetables and
egg garnish the platter of Avocado with Shrimp Rémoulade.

Avocado with Shrimp Rémoulade

¼ cup tarragon vinegar
2 tablespoons horseradish mustard
1 tablespoon catsup
1½ teaspoons paprika
½ teaspoon salt
¼ teaspoon cayenne pepper
½ cup salad oil
¼ cup minced celery
¼ cup minced green onion and tops
2 pounds fresh or frozen shrimp
   in shells, cooked, peeled,
   and deveined
4 medium avocados
Lettuce

Prepare Rémoulade Sauce by combining vinegar, mustard, catsup, paprika, salt, and cayenne pepper in a small bowl. Slowly add salad oil, beating mixture constantly with rotary or electric beater. Stir in celery and onion. Pour over shrimp. Cover and marinate shrimp in refrigerator for 4 to 5 hours.

Line serving platter with lettuce. At serving time halve, pit, and peel avocados; place cut side up on lettuce-lined platter. Lift shrimp out of Rémoulade Sauce and arrange 5 or 6 on each avocado half. If desired, serve with cooked, chilled asparagus spears; cooked carrot strips; sliced, cooked, chilled beets; and sliced hard-cooked eggs. Pass remaining Rémoulade Sauce. Makes 8 servings.

B

BABA *(bä′ buh)*—A spongelike cake made with yeast and mixed with raisins, then baked in a tall, slightly flared mold or in individual molds. The freshly baked cake is turned out and soaked with a sugar and water syrup, usually flavored with rum, kirsch, or brandy. When the syrup used for soaking is flavored with rum the finished product is called Baba au Rhum.

The origin of the baba is credited to King Stanislas Leczinski, the gourmet and Polish king, but some say that he just adapted a new way to eat *kugelhoff* (a sugar-dusted Central European cake) by drizzling rum over the cake, then flaming it. He named this specialty after a hero in one of his favorite books, Ali Baba from *Thousand and One Nights.*

The baba was introduced to Paris in the early 1800s. Later the recipe was changed: raisins were omitted from the dough, the shape was changed to a ring mold, and the syrup altered. It also got another new name, Brillat-Savarin, in memory of a French gourmet; now it is simply called savarin and the center is usually filled with whipped cream or a soft custard and is covered with a fruit glaze.

As we know them today, some babas contain raisins, others do not. Some are large and some individual servings. And there are also available ready-to-serve tiny babas in rum syrup in cans or jars.

Baba au Rhum

In large mixer bowl combine 1 package active dry yeast and 2 cups sifted all-purpose flour. Heat ½ cup butter, ⅓ cup milk, ¼ cup sugar, and ½ teaspoon salt in saucepan just till warm, stirring occasionally to melt butter. Add to flour mixture in mixing bowl.

Add 4 eggs. Beat at low speed with electric mixer for ½ minute, scraping sides of bowl constantly. Beat 3 minutes at high speed. Stir in ½ cup golden raisins and ¼ cup currants. Cover; let rise in warm place till double, about 1 to 1½ hours. Stir down batter.

Spoon into well-greased 1½-quart baba mold. Cover; let rise till almost double, about 45 minutes. Bake at 350° for 25 to 30 minutes or till done. Cool 10 minutes; remove from mold.

Combine 1 cup sugar and ¾ cup water in saucepan; bring to boiling. Remove from heat and cool to lukewarm. Stir in ½ cup rum. Spoon syrup over cake, a little at a time, till all the syrup is absorbed.

A number of modern variations are used in the making of babas. Preparation time is shortened by using a hot roll mix or cake mix as the basis for the dough. When a tall baba mold isn't available, a ring mold or individual-serving molds can be used. And a tangy orange syrup can be substituted as the "soaking" liquid.

Tangy orange flavors an easy baba version. Hot roll mix is the quick beginning for Baba au Orange and frozen orange juice concentrate makes the glowing beauty a special dessert.

Baba au Orange

Easy version of a gourmet treat—

1 13¾-ounce package hot roll mix
⅓ cup sugar
6 tablespoons butter or margarine, softened
2 eggs
1 6-ounce can frozen orange juice concentrate
1 cup sugar
1 cup water
Sliced almonds

Prepare mix following package directions. Stir in ⅓ cup sugar and butter. Thoroughly beat in eggs, one at a time. Cover; let rise till double, about 1 hour. Turn into well-greased 6½-cup ring mold. Let rise till almost double, 30 to 45 minutes. Bake at 400° for 30 minutes. If necessary, cover with foil last 10 minutes to prevent overbrowning.

Meanwhile, in a saucepan combine the frozen concentrate, 1 cup sugar, and water. Bring to a rolling boil. Remove from heat. Turn baba out in a shallow baking pan. Immediately spoon hot orange syrup over. Baste with syrup till all is absorbed. Garnish top with almonds. Serve cool. Makes 6 to 8 servings.

Freshly baked baba is soaked with a hot sugar and water syrup making the sponge-like cake delightfully sweet and very moist.

Orange Babas

Individual babas made from a cake mix—

1 package 1-layer-size yellow
    cake mix
½ cup sugar
½ cup water
⅓ cup frozen orange juice
    concentrate, thawed
Sliced almonds

Prepare cake mix according to package directions. Turn batter into 8 well-greased 5-ounce custard cups. Bake at 350° for 25 minutes.

Meanwhile, combine sugar, water, and orange juice concentrate in a saucepan. Bring to a rolling boil; remove from heat. Let cakes cool 5 minutes, then remove from cups and place in shallow serving dishes.

Drizzle hot orange syrup over babas. Cool. Serve with whipped cream, if desired. Garnish with almonds. Makes 8 servings.

BACARDI—A well-known dry rum of the West Indies. Bacardi is also the name for a delicate-pink cocktail based on light rum, grenadine, lime juice, and sometimes sugar. (See *Cocktail, Rum, Wines and Spirits* for additional information.)

Bacardi Cocktail

2 ounces light rum
2 tablespoons grenadine
2 teaspoons lime juice
1½ to 2 cups crushed ice

Combine all ingredients in a cocktail shaker. Cover and shake well. Add 1 drop red food coloring, if desired. Strain into cocktail glasses. Makes 2 servings.

BACON—Salted, smoked meat from the back or sides of a hog. Its distinctive flavor and tantalizing aroma have made it a breakfast favorite and a popular seasoning since the early pioneer days in America.

Bacon is processed in the packing plant before it comes to market. The pork side or back is trimmed and squared into shape and the meat cured. Curing formulas vary to give different flavors, such as the maple flavor. Next, it's hung and smoked with special woods which give bacon that typical aroma. Bacon is then chilled and formed into a shape suitable for cutting into uniform slices. In the last stage, the slabs are sliced and packaged.

Bacon is a source of food energy and contains modest amounts of protein, B vitamins, and minerals. One crisp-cooked slice yields about 50 calories.

The homemaker has a choice in the thickness of the sliced bacon she buys. Regular packaged bacon is cut to yield 16 to 22 slices per pound. Thick-slice bacon will have approximately 12 slices per pound. Irregular shaped pieces are packaged and labeled "ends and pieces."

Bacon is also sold in slabs. This the meatman will derind and slice on request. Cured and smoked bacon squares which come from the jowl are also marketed. Prefried bacon widely used by the military brings its convenience to the consumer too.

Tastes like a holiday meal

Canadian Bacon Stack-Ups combines Canadian-style bacon, spicy whipped sweet potatoes, and cranberry sauce for a royal feast. →

Bacon is sold in slices or in slabs. Its savory flavor makes bacon popular as a side dish, for an ingredient, and for a seasoning.

Bacon Squares (Jowl Bacon) can be sliced and cooked like regular bacon, or cubed for cooking with vegetables for seasoning.

Canadian-Style Bacon, available in slices or pieces, is usually fully cooked and has no waste. Delicious either baked or fried.

Finally, there are the lean, round slices of cured and smoked pork loin known as Canadian-style bacon.

When buying bacon, select meat with firm, white fat that is evenly ribboned with bright pinkish red lean. Too much fat will cause excessive shrinkage and too much lean will result in tough bacon.

Keep bacon in the original package or wrap in foil and store in the refrigerator for six or seven days. Avoid exposing to air or light which can result in quality loss. Prolonged freezer storage of bacon also leads to quality loss. One month at 0° is generally considered maximum for greatest eating enjoyment. (See also *Pork*.)

Bacon Butter

    ½ cup butter or margarine,
        softened
    ¾ teaspoon prepared mustard
    4 slices bacon, crisp-cooked and
        crumbled

Cream butter till light and fluffy. Blend in mustard and bacon. Makes ½ to ⅔ cup.

Canadian Bacon Stack-Ups

    1 cup whole cranberry sauce
    2 tablespoons light corn syrup
    1 17-ounce can sweet potatoes,
        drained
    1 tablespoon butter or margarine,
        melted
    1 tablespoon brown sugar
    ¼ teaspoon ground ginger
    1 pound *unsliced* Canadian-style
        bacon

Combine cranberry sauce and corn syrup in bowl. Beat potatoes, butter, brown sugar, and ginger with electric mixer till light and fluffy. Slice bacon into 12 pieces. Arrange *six* slices in baking dish and spread *half* the potato mixture equally on each slice.

Cover with remaining bacon slices and top each with a mound of remaining potato mixture. Drizzle cranberry sauce over stacks. Bake at 350° for 45 minutes, basting once or twice with sauce in dish. Makes 6 servings.

Separate cold bacon slices quickly and without tearing. Slip rubber spatula under end of slice; "cut" and lift lengthwise.

To fry bacon, place strips in cold skillet and cook over moderately low heat 6 to 8 minutes, turning often. Do not let smoke.

To broil bacon, arrange slices on cold rack of broiler pan. Broil 3 to 5 inches from heat, turning once. Watch bacon closely.

To oven-bake, place bacon slices on a rack in shallow pan. Bake at 400° 10 minutes. Do not turn—easy way to cook for a crowd.

Bacon Crisps

Unusual way to dress up bacon for lunch—

¼ cup evaporated milk
2 tablespoons catsup
1 teaspoon Worcestershire sauce
   Dash monosodium glutamate
8 slices bacon
⅔ cup cornflake crumbs

Combine evaporated milk, catsup, Worcestershire sauce, monosodium glutamate, and dash pepper. Brush on bacon; dip slices in crumbs. Place bacon on rack in shallow baking pan. Bake at 375° about 20 minutes or till bacon is crisp. Makes 4 servings.

Bacon Big Boys

2 large French rolls
4 slices sharp natural Cheddar
   cheese
4 frankfurters
6 to 8 slices bacon

Split rolls lengthwise; if tops are rounded, trim slightly. Spread inside of tops with prepared mustard. Arrange 2 cheese slices and 2 frankfurters on bottom half of each. Replace tops.

Wrap 3 or 4 bacon slices spiral fashion around each roll; secure with picks. Place, top down, on rack in shallow pan. Bake at 400° for 5 to 8 minutes. Turn; bake 5 to 8 minutes more. Makes 2 servings.

Crab-Bacon Rolls

A "meaty" appetizer—

¼ cup tomato juice
1 well-beaten egg
1 7½-ounce can crab meat,
    drained, flaked, and
    cartilage removed
½ cup fine dry bread crumbs
1 tablespoon snipped parsley
1 tablespoon lemon juice
¼ teaspoon salt
¼ teaspoon Worcestershire sauce
    Dash pepper
        • • •
9 slices bacon, cut in half

Mix tomato juice and egg. Add crab, bread crumbs, parsley, lemon juice, salt, Worcestershire, and pepper; mix thoroughly. Shape into 18 rolls, about 2 inches long. Wrap each roll with ½ slice bacon; fasten with wooden picks.

Broil rolls 5 inches from heat about 10 minutes, turning often to brown evenly. Serve immediately. Makes 18 appetizers.

Scalloped Bacon and Eggs

Sparked-up bacon and eggs—a standard combination, served in an entirely different way—

¼ cup chopped onion
2 tablespoons butter or margarine
2 tablespoons all-purpose flour
1½ cups milk
4 ounces sharp process American
    cheese, shredded (1 cup)
        • • •
6 hard-cooked eggs, sliced
1½ cups crushed potato chips
10 to 12 slices bacon, crisp-
    cooked and crumbled

Cook onion in butter till tender, but not brown; blend in flour. Add milk. Cook, stirring constantly, till mixture is thickened and bubbly. Add cheese; stir till melted.

Place a layer of egg slices in 10x6x1½-inch baking dish. Cover with *half* the cheese sauce, *half* the potato chips, and *half* the bacon. Repeat layers. Bake at 350° for 15 to 20 minutes or till heated through. Serves 4.

Bacon-Macaroni Bake

Serve with a crisp salad and favorite vegetable—

1 7-ounce package elbow macaroni
½ pound sliced bacon
½ cup chopped onion
4 ounces sharp process American
    cheese, grated (1 cup)
1 10¾-ounce can condensed
    tomato soup
1 cup milk

Cook macaroni using package directions; drain. Cook bacon till crisp; drain, reserving 2 tablespoons drippings. Crumble bacon. Cook onion in reserved bacon drippings till tender.

Combine macaroni, bacon, onion, cheese, tomato soup, and milk. Turn into 2-quart casserole. Bake at 375° for 45 minutes or till heated through. Makes 6 servings.

Avocado-Bacon Sandwich

Dressed with smooth blue cheese—

¼ cup buttermilk
½ cup mayonnaise or salad
    dressing
2 tablespoons chopped onion
½ teaspoon Worcestershire sauce
    Dash garlic salt
2 ounces blue cheese, crumbled
    (½ cup)
        • • •
6 slices rye bread, toasted
    Leaf lettuce
12 slices bacon, crisp-cooked and
    drained
3 medium avocados, seeded,
    peeled, and sliced
1 lemon, cut in 6 wedges

Put buttermilk, mayonnaise, onion, Worcestershire, and garlic salt into blender container; add *half* the blue cheese. Cover and run on high speed till smooth. Stir in remaining cheese. Spread each piece of toast generously with blue cheese dressing mixture.

Top each sandwich with lettuce leaves, 2 slices cooked bacon, and avocado slices. Drizzle additional dressing over top; garnish with lemon wedges. Makes 6 servings.

Bacon Cornettes

Bits of crisp bacon flavor cornmeal muffins—

10 to 12 slices bacon
1 cup sifted all-purpose flour
¼ cup sugar
4 teaspoons baking powder
¾ teaspoon salt
1 cup yellow cornmeal
. . .
2 well-beaten eggs
1 cup milk
¼ cup salad oil

Cook bacon till crisp; drain and crumble. Sift together flour, sugar, baking powder, and salt; stir in cornmeal. Add eggs, milk, and oil. Beat till *just* smooth, about 1 minute (do not over-beat). Stir in bacon.

Fill greased muffin pans about ⅔ full. If desired, top with a few additional bits of uncooked bacon. Bake at 425° for 20 to 25 minutes or till done. Makes 12 muffins.

Bean and Bacon Slaw

4 slices bacon
¼ cup chopped onion
⅓ cup wine vinegar
1 teaspoon sugar
½ teaspoon salt
Dash pepper
. . .
2 cups shredded cabbage
1 17-ounce can baby limas, drained
1 3-ounce can sliced mushrooms, drained

Fry bacon in skillet till crisp. Drain bacon, reserving drippings; crumble and set aside. Cook onion in reserved drippings in skillet till lightly browned. Stir in vinegar, sugar, salt, and pepper; simmer several minutes.

Combine shredded cabbage, baby limas, and sliced mushroom in bowl. Pour vinegar mixture over cabbage mixture and toss. Sprinkle with crumbled bacon. Makes 6 servings.

Bacon Big Boys are real he-man sandwiches for hungry appetites. Frankfurters and sharp Cheddar cheese inside French rolls are all bound together with sizzling strips of bacon.

BAGEL *(bā′ guhl)*—A handmade yeast roll twisted into a small doughnut shape. It is occasionally called a water doughnut.

The nonsweet dough is made with yeast, wheat flour, water, and sometimes eggs and onion. Bagels are simmered in water before they are baked giving the crust a glazed appearance. A bland flavor and chewy, white interior is typical of this roll.

Bagels are associated with Jewish cuisine and are often eaten with lox (smoked salmon) and cream cheese. (See *Bread, Jewish Cookery* for additional information.)

BAG PUDDING—A pudding made by wrapping dough in a floured cloth then cooking it in boiling water for several hours. There are two basic bag puddings: a dessert pudding made with fruit such as berries and a main dish pudding which contains a meat mixture enclosed in a doughy crust.

BAGUETTE *(ba get′)*—A rod-shaped French bread. This long cylindrical loaf is about two feet long yet quite small in diameter. The bread is notable for its thick, crisp, golden crust. (See also *French Bread.*)

BAIN-MARIE *(ban′ muh rē′)*—A French utensil similar to a double boiler. A pan containing the food is set into a larger pan or casserole, half filled with hot water. Because the two pans do not fit together as a double boiler does, the water remains near the boiling point but does not boil over or steam. A larger version of the bain-marie that resembles a steam table, has several openings for pots or pans with hot water or steam circulating around and under the food containers.

The bain-marie is used to cook delicate dishes such as custards, puddings, mousses, and fish or meat loaves. This method of cooking without direct heat prevents the food from curdling or disintegrating.

The bain-marie may also be used, as is the double boiler—to keep food warm. Purée, béarnaise, hollandaise, allemande, and white or brown gravy can be kept hot while retaining the eating quality.

The literal translation of bain-marie is "bath of Maria" but the translation "water bath" is the most appropriate in reference to food preparation.

BAKE—To cook by dry heat, covered or uncovered, in an oven or oven-type appliance, under coals, or on heated metal or stone. Cooking meat uncovered is called roasting except for ham which is baked.

Oven Chart

Very slow oven	250°-275°
Slow oven	300°-325°
Moderate oven	350°-375°
Hot oven	400°-425°
Very hot oven	450°-475°
Extremely hot oven	500°-525°

BAKED ALASKA—A dessert made with cake and ice cream covered with meringue and baked or broiled until the meringue is golden. The ice cream will remain firm.

The origin of this glamorous dessert dates back to the early 1800s when it was first known as Alaska-Florida, presumedly because of the contrasting cold and hot nature of the ingredients. The name "baked Alaska" has now been adopted.

The dessert is made from a cake layer which is at least one inch thick and should extend one half to one inch beyond the ice cream edges. Sherbet or a combination of ice cream or sherbet flavors can be used as well as ice cream. A soft meringue is spread thickly and completely over the ice cream and cake. It's extremely important that the meringue meets the edges of the cake to form a seal all around the ice cream. The alaska is baked in a very hot oven or broiled until the meringue is browned.

Tiny air cells in the meringue act as an insulator to keep the heat away from the ice cream, but once cut baked Alaska must be served quickly because the warmth of the room air will melt the ice cream.

Do a magic trick

Serve hot and cold Mile-High Mocha Alaska → right from the oven. Everyone will be convinced a magician has performed this feat.

Strawberry Sunshine Pie is made in a pastry shell for a baked alaska variation. The lemon sherbet and fresh strawberry filling stay cool while the fluffy meringue is browned.

To save last-minute preparation, baked Alaska can be assembled ahead and frozen. At serving time, whisk the alaska into the oven to brown. (See *Dessert, Ice Cream, Meringue* for additional information.)

Strawberry Sunshine Pie

    **Plain Pastry for 1 9–inch crust
      (See *Pastry*)**
1 **pint lemon sherbet, softened**
3 **egg whites**
½ **teaspoon vanilla**
¼ **teaspoon cream of tartar**
7 **tablespoons sugar**
1 **quart fresh strawberries,
    sliced**

Prepare Plain Pastry according to recipe directions. Fit pastry into 9-inch pie plate trimming ½ to 1 inch beyond edge. Fold under and flute edge of pastry. Bake at 450° for 10 to 12 minutes or till golden. Cool completely.

Spread sherbet in bottom of pastry shell; freeze till firm, 4 to 5 hours or overnight. Beat egg whites with vanilla and cream of tartar till soft peaks form. Gradually add *6 tablespoons* sugar, beating till stiff and glossy peaks form.

Sweeten strawberries with remaining sugar. Working quickly, arrange strawberries over lemon sherbet. Spread meringue over berries being careful to seal meringue to edge of pastry.

Place pie on cutting board and bake at 475° for 5 or 6 minutes or till meringue is golden. Cut in wedges with sharp knife dipped in water. Serve immediately. Makes 6 to 8 servings.

Spread plenty of meringue around the edge where ice cream and cake meet. This seal keeps the ice cream firm while being baked.

Mile-High Mocha Alaska

    2 pints chocolate ice cream
    1 to 2 pints coffee ice cream
    1 Brownie Layer
    5 egg whites
    ⅔ cup sugar

For a mold, line deep 1½-quart bowl with foil, allowing 1 inch extra to extend over edge of bowl. Stir chocolate ice cream to soften, *slightly;* using back of spoon spread a layer about 1 inch thick over bottom and sides of foil liner. Place mold in freezer. Stir coffee ice cream to soften *slightly*. Remove mold from freezer. Pack coffee ice cream into center of mold. Cover with foil, pressing to smooth top. Freeze till *firm*.

For Brownie Layer, prepare one recipe Cake Brownies (See *Brownie*), baking in greased 8-inch *round* pan. Cool; remove from pan.

To assemble Alaska, place cooled Brownie Layer on cookie sheet or wooden cutting board. Let ice cream mold stand at room temperature to loosen from sides while preparing meringue.

Beat egg whites till soft peaks form; gradually add sugar, beating till stiff peaks form. Remove foil from top of ice cream; invert ice cream mold onto Brownie Layer. Lift off bowl and peel foil off the ice cream mold.

Working quickly cover ice cream mold and Brownie Layer with meringue. Swirl meringue into peaks and seal around edges of cake.

Place cookie sheet or wooden board on lowest rack in oven at once and bake at 500° for 3 minutes or till meringue is golden brown. Let stand a few minutes for easier cutting. Cut in wedge-shaped slices. Serves 12.

Baked Alaska

    1 1-inch layer sponge *or* layer
       cake
    1 quart brick of ice cream *or*
       2 pint bricks ice cream
    5 egg whites
    ⅔ cup sugar
       Sugar

Trim cake 1-inch larger on all sides than brick ice cream; place cake on wooden cutting board. (Keep ice cream frozen.) Beat egg whites till soft peaks form; gradually add ⅔ cup sugar, beating till stiff peaks form.

Center brick of ice cream on cake layer (place pints side-by-side if used). Spread meringue over ice cream and cake, sealing to edges of cake all around. Swirl in peaks. Sprinkle lightly with sugar. Bake at 500° till meringue is golden, about 3 minutes. Slice and serve immediately. Makes 8 servings.

BAKERS' CHEESE—A skim milk cheese resembling cottage cheese but softer in texture and sharper in flavor. It is used primarily in commercial baking of cheese cakes and pastries. (See also *Cheese*.)

BAKING DISH—A glass or ceramic utensil capable of withstanding oven temperatures. Shapes vary from casseroles to shallow dishes. Sizes are measured in inches or quarts; always use exact size specified.

Because glass and ceramic hold more heat than metal does, the oven temperature should be lowered 25 degrees when using glass and ceramic dishes where the recipe does not specify glass. (See also *Pots and Pans*.)

BAKING PAN—A metal utensil used for oven cooking made of lightweight aluminum or stainless steel. A good baking pan should cook food evenly and thoroughly. (See also *Pots and Pans*.)

BAKING POWDER—A chemical leavening consisting of a mixture of an acid-reacting material and sodium bicarbonate (baking soda). A starch, usually cornstarch, is added to standardize the mixture and keep it dry. This prevents the acid and soda from reacting with each other in the can.

When liquid and baking powder are mixed in the preparation of baked foods, carbon dioxide gas bubbles are trapped in the mixture. This causes the dough to rise and to become light and porous. The heat applied during baking is necessary to stabilize this porous structure.

Although this principle of leavening by using baking soda with an acid salt was familiar to homemakers before baking powder was on the retail market, the leavening of baked foods was a hit or miss affair. Homemakers talked of either having good luck or poor luck with the week's baking. There is little science, however, to their theory of luck. Failures were more likely caused by improper leavening than luck. Variations in measuring the amount of baking soda and cream of tartar used in the recipe, or leaving the measurement to guesswork were more often the cause of the poor baked products.

Although the first formulas for baking powder were developed in the United States in the 1850s, it seems unlikely, because of poor transportation facilities, that baking powder was widely available in the United States until after the Civil War. Early baking powder formulas included various acids mixed with baking soda and starch or flour. Sometimes the baking soda and the acid were packaged in separate containers and accompanied by instructions and a wooden measuring device.

Types of baking powder: There are four types of baking powder: tartrate, phosphate, anhydrous phosphate, and sodium aluminum sulfate-phosphate. All four types contain a starch and baking soda but the acid salt ingredient differs.

Tartrate baking powders contain the acid ingredients cream of tartar and tartaric acid. The first baking powders sold were this type. These baking powders are known as single-action because they are quick to react as soon as moistened. Much of the gas is given off during mixing and the remainder is released during baking. Because all of this happens as a continuous reaction, speedy handling of the batter from bowl to oven is essential so that as much of the rising action as possible takes place in the oven.

Phosphate baking powders contain calcium or sodium phosphate as the acid salt. These release a fair amount (but not as much as tartrate baking powders) of the carbon dioxide in the cold mixture. The rest is released during baking.

Anhydrous phosphate baking powders have anhydrous monocalcium phosphate as their acid ingredient. This acid salt has been treated to slow down the rate at which it dissolves. Little carbon dioxide is released during mixing. Carbon dioxide production accelerates early in the baking period. This type of baking powder is not sold extensively on the retail market but is widely used in packaged mixes.

Sodium aluminum sulfate-phosphate baking powders contain sodium aluminum sulfate and calcium phosphate, as acid salts. Since sodium aluminum sulfate reacts slowly with baking soda, the phosphate is added to speed up the reaction.

Baking powders of this type are considered double-action because the phosphate reacts with the baking soda while the mixture is cold, whereas heat is necessary before the sulfate reacts. About 85 percent of baking powders sold on the retail market are sodium aluminum sulfate-phosphate.

Unless another type of baking powder is specified, a double-action product is intended in most recipes.

Baking powder is a small ingredient in a recipe yet it has great influence on the shape, volume, grain, texture, and lightness of the finished product.

Accurate level measurement of baking powder is very important. The exact amount a recipe calls for gives the product the best texture and volume. Too little baking powder makes baked foods heavy and compact. Too much can cause over-rising followed by collapse, coarse loose texture, and often a lingering baking powder taste. As a general guide, one to two teaspoons of baking powder should be used for every cup of flour in a recipe.

Orange Celebration Cake

⅓ cup butter or margarine
⅓ cup shortening
2 teaspoons grated orange peel
1½ cups sugar
3 eggs
2½ cups sifted cake flour
2½ teaspoons baking powder
1 teaspoon salt
1 cup orange juice
Orange Filling
Seven Minute Frosting (See *Frosting* for recipe)

Cream together butter, shortening, and peel. Gradually add sugar, creaming till light. Add eggs, one at a time, beating well after each. Sift together dry ingredients and add alternately with orange juice to creamed mixture, beating after each addition. Bake in 2 greased and lightly floured 9x1½-inch round pans at 350° for 25 to 30 minutes or till done. Cool 10 minutes; remove from pans. Cool.

Fill layers with *Orange Filling:* Combine ⅔ cup sugar and 3 tablespoons all-purpose flour in saucepan. Add 1 cup orange juice and 2 egg yolks. Cook and stir till mixture boils; cook 1 minute. Stir in 2 tablespoons butter; cool. Frost cake with Seven Minute Frosting.

Onion Biscuits

¼ cup finely chopped onion
1 tablespoon shortening
1½ cups sifted all-purpose flour
1½ teaspoons baking powder
½ teaspoon celery seed
¼ cup shortening
1 slightly beaten egg
⅓ cup milk

Cook onion in 1 tablespoon shortening till tender. Sift together flour, baking powder, and ½ teaspoon salt; stir in celery seed. Cut in shortening till mixture resembles coarse crumbs. Add onion, egg, and milk all at once and stir just till dough follows fork around bowl.

Turn out on lightly floured surface and knead gently ½ minute. Pat or roll ½ inch thick. Cut with floured 1¾-inch cutter. Bake on ungreased baking sheet at 425° for 12 minutes or till done. Makes 12 biscuits.

Since baking powder was first introduced in the middle of the 19th century, housewives have found it more convenient and reliable than baking soda alone. Today most recipes, though by no means all, use baking powder or baking powder plus additional soda in place of baking soda by itself. (See also *Leavening Agent*.)

BAKING SODA—Pure sodium bicarbonate. Chemical leavening is almost universally produced by carbon dioxide gas resulting from the reaction of sodium bicarbonate (baking soda) with an acid.

When sodium bicarbonate is heated, it gives off carbon dioxide gas and leaves sodium carbonate. In baked foods this compound has an objectionable taste which is eliminated by combining the baking soda with an acid at the time the batter is mixed. This acid ingredient can be present in the food or in the baking powder.

Soured milk, buttermilk, sour cream, molasses, vinegar, and fruit juices are some of the acid-containing foods used with baking soda in baking. Since the acidity of these foods varies, it is difficult to know how much baking soda to add. Baking powder contains a standardized amount of baking soda and acid salt so takes much of the guesswork out of baking.

If the carbon dioxide evolved by the reaction of an acid food and baking soda is to be used for leavening, the soda must be sifted with the dry ingredients. If it is mixed with the acid ingredient before adding, the gas will be lost.

A pinch of baking soda is sometimes suggested as a means of keeping green vegetables green as they cook or of making dried beans tender more quickly. Nutritionists frown on this practice, however, because it hastens the loss of thiamine and makes the vegetables mushy.

Baking soda is used in various types of chocolate cake because of the way in which it affects the brown color. The most soda is used in Devil's food cake, giving it a rich mahogany color when soured milk is an ingredient or a deep red when sweet milk is used, instead. The use of baking soda in any type of chocolate cake results in a cake that is darker than one made with all baking powder.

Prize Chocolate Cake

    1 cup shortening
    2 cups sugar
    2 teaspoons vanilla
    4 1-ounce squares unsweetened
        chocolate, melted and cooled
    5 eggs
 2¼ cups sifted cake flour
    1 teaspoon baking soda
    1 teaspoon salt
    1 cup sour milk *or buttermilk*

Cream shortening and sugar till light and fluffy. Blend in vanilla and cooled chocolate. Add eggs, one at a time, beating well after each addition. Sift together flour, baking soda, and salt; add to creamed mixture alternately with milk, beating after each addition. Bake in 2 greased and lightly-floured 9x1½-inch round pans at 350° for 35 to 40 minutes or till done. Cool. Frost.

Spiced Chocolate Cake

    ⅔ cup shortening
    2 cups sifted all-purpose flour
    2 cups sugar
    1 teaspoon baking powder
    1 teaspoon baking soda
    1 teaspoon salt
    1 teaspoon ground cloves
    1 teaspoon ground cinnamon
    1 teaspoon instant coffee powder
 1½ cups buttermilk
    3 eggs
    4 1-ounce squares unsweetened
        chocolate, melted and cooled
    1 teaspoon vanilla
        Seven Minute Frosting (See
        Frosting for recipe)

Place shortening in mixing bowl. Sift in flour, sugar, baking powder, baking soda, salt, ground cloves, ground cinnamon, and instant coffee powder. Add *1 cup* of the buttermilk; mix till all flour is moistened. Beat mixture vigorously 2 minutes.

Stir in remaining buttermilk, eggs, cooled chocolate, and vanilla. Beat 2 minutes longer. Bake in greased and lightly floured 13x9x2-inch baking dish at 350° for 40 minutes or till done. Cool. Frost with Seven Minute Frosting.

Butterscotch Cookies

    ½ cup butter or margarine
    ⅔ cup brown sugar
    1 egg
 1⅓ cups sifted all-purpose
        flour
    ¾ teaspoon baking soda
    ¾ teaspoon vanilla
    ⅓ cup chopped walnuts

Melt butter in 2-quart saucepan; add sugar and mix well. Add egg; beat till light colored. Sift flour with baking soda; stir into egg mixture. Add vanilla and walnuts. Chill.

Roll into small balls. Bake on ungreased cookie sheet at 375° for 7 to 10 minutes. Remove from cookie sheet at once. Makes 3 dozen.

Aside from its baking properties, sodium bicarbonate is a versatile cleansing agent. Many people use it instead of a commercial toothpaste. Soda is also used to clean painted walls, plastic tablecloths, windows, costume jewelry, and fine crystal. Baking soda will rid hands of fishy odors, take the soreness out of sunburn, clear refrigerators of stale odors, and sooth the itch or sting of insect bites. (See also *Leavening Agent*.)

BAKLAVA, BAKALAWA (*bä′ kluh vä*)—A Greek and Middle Eastern dessert made of wafer-thin pastry sheets filled with nuts, butter, and honey, and covered with honey or a sugar syrup. These pastries are usually cut into diamond-shaped pieces for serving. (See also *Greek Cookery*.)

BALM—Any of various aromatic plants similar to mint. Lemon balm is the best known variety and the word balm usually refers to this herb.

Lemon balm is a hardy perennial herb which reaches a height of 1½ to 2 feet. It has broad, dark green, crinkled leaves, which have a fragrant lemon odor and a faint lemon flavor. The pale yellow flowers grow in clusters. Lemon balm thrives in all temperate climates and is often used as an attractive garden border.

The ancient Greeks and Orientals crushed lemon balm and used it to flavor their tea and wine drinks. Tea made from balm leaves was valued by the Arabs because it made "the heart merry and joyful."

Many medicinal properties have been attributed to this herb. In ancient Greece, balm leaves were used in medicinal drinks as remedies for scorpion or dog bites. The leaves were also applied to the body to relieve the pain of gout, draw out congestion, and "leave one light-headed." In some European countries, fresh balm leaves are still used as a remedy for fainting and virus cold fevers.

Although the leaves and tender sprigs lend a subtle, charming lemon flavor to lemonade, teas, meats, poultry, sauces, stuffings, soups, and salads, the use of lemon balm has declined in the United States. This decline is possibly due to the year round availability of lemons. Today the prime use of balm is in the industrial manufacture of perfumes and liqueurs. (See also *Herbs*.)

BAMBOO SHOOT—The edible young sprout from certain varieties of the tropical plant, bamboo. Since only the young shoots are tender, bamboo shoots must be harvested before they become mature. To keep the shoots tender and fit for consumption longer, the young plants are covered with hills of earth. The shoots are then cut as soon as the tiny tip appears through the top of the mound.

Although the supply is more abundant in autumn, bamboo shoots are harvested the year round. Each shoot is covered with a thick, tight, overlapping, spiny sheath that must be stripped off before the succulent inner flesh of the bamboo shoot can be cooked and eaten.

In the Orient where they grow, bamboo shoots are used as a vegetable and served similar to asparagus. Bamboo shoots are also salted and eaten with rice; pickled; candied; and used in meat dishes.

Fresh bamboo shoots are available only near the growing area, but cooked, canned shoots are imported from Taiwan and Japan and are available in markets in this country. These shoots have a flavor somewhat resembling the flavor of artichokes and are most frequently used as an ingredient in oriental dishes.

Chicken Almond

      2 cups skinned uncooked chicken
        breasts cut in thin strips
        (about 2 whole breasts)
  ¼ cup shortening or salad oil
      3 cups chicken broth
      2 5-ounce cans bamboo shoots,
        drained and diced
      2 5-ounce cans water chestnuts,
        drained and sliced
      2 cups diced celery
      1 cup diced bok choy (Chinese
        chard) *or* romaine
      2 tablespoons soy sauce
      2 teaspoons monosodium glutamate
  ⅓ cup cornstarch
  ½ cup cold water
  ½ cup halved almonds, toasted
            • • •
      Hot cooked rice

In large heavy skillet quickly cook chicken in hot shortening or salad oil. Add chicken broth, bamboo shoots, water chestnuts, celery, bok choy *or* romaine, soy sauce, and monosodium glutamate; mix thoroughly. Bring to boiling; cover and cook over low heat for 5 minutes. Vegetables should be tender yet still crisp.

Blend cornstarch and cold water; add to chicken mixture. Cook, stirring constantly, till mixture thickens and bubbles. Salt to taste. Garnish with almonds. Serve immediately over hot cooked rice. Makes 6 servings.

Note: High heat and quick stirring are essential; avoid overcooking.

If part of a can is leftover, bamboo shoots can be kept for quite awhile in the refrigerator. To store leftovers, place the shoots in a clean container, cover them with cold water, and seal the container with an airtight lid. Place the leftovers in the warmest part of the refrigerator and change the water at least every other day. (See also *Oriental Cookery*.)

BAMBOO SKEWERS—Slender sticks, made from slivered bamboo. These skewers vary in length from 4 to 10 inches and are popularly used for the hibachi cooking of kebabs. Food strung on the bamboo skewers are rotated over the hibachi coals.

BANANA—The elongated yellow- or red-rinded fruit of the tropical banana plant. These popular fruits, like many other foods, have been eating favorites for thousands of years. In fact, history suggests that bananas were one of the very first plants to be cultivated by man. The evidence indicates they were known in southern Asia during prehistoric times and, in all likelihood, probably originated in the East Indies. Bananas were also cultivated in India some 4,000 years ago.

Two ancient names for the banana give an indication of the esteem in which the fruit was held. One name translates as "fruit of the wise man" and another means the "fruit of paradise."

Explorers and traders are credited with carrying banana plants to the Near East and to Africa. Spanish missionaries then introduced them to the tropical Americas after Columbus made his voyages and discovered the banana in that area.

The two-fruit combination in Strawberry-Banana Mold has long been a refreshing favorite with children and adults alike.

How bananas are produced: Although banana plants resemble trees, they are, nevertheless, plants with trunk-like stems made of leafstalks wrapped tightly together in long, stiff bundles. At maturity (12 to 15 months), the plants have grown to a height of from 10 to 18 feet. The plant loaded with fruit is an interesting sight because the fruit appears to grow upside down.

Bananas prefer loose, well-drained soil and humid, tropical weather. Thus the bananas purchased in American markets all year are imported from plantations in tropical countries, mainly Central America, South America, and the West Indies where they are an important crop.

Unlike most fruits, bananas are harvested in bunches when mature but still green since flavor decreases as a banana ripens on the tree. Once picked, the fruit or "hands" are removed from the bunch, broken into clusters, and packed in fiberboard cartons. While on board the cargo ships the bananas are stored in atmospherically controlled rooms.

Similar handling care and storage control protect the quality of the fruit as it is transported across the United States. Upon reaching final destination, the fruit is placed in ripening rooms which have scientifically-controlled moisture content and temperature. During ripening under these conditions much of the starch in the bananas is changed to sugar.

Nutritional value: About one-fourth of the bananas' food value is in the form of carbohydrates, mainly sugar. Bananas contain vitamins A and C plus all of the B vitamin group. One 6-inch banana contains about 85 calories.

Types of bananas: Some 300 varieties of banana exist but three main types are commonly marketed. Two of these are eaten and used like other fruits. The yellow, smooth-skinned banana is the type most frequently seen in grocery stores. Red banana, a lesser-known variety, is shorter and thicker than the yellow one, but has similar flavor and texture.

Plantain, the third type, resembles the yellow banana in shape and color but is thicker and larger. The hard, starchy plantain however, is eaten as a cooked vegetable rather than as a fruit. It is a staple in Central American kitchens.

How to select: Choosing good bananas requires familiarization with the bananas themselves and their popularity with your family. Special terminology, for instance, describes bananas as seen in markets.

A bunch of bananas is the whole growth of fruit as picked from the plant, while a hand of bananas is a natural grouping of 6 to 15 bananas within the bunch. The bananas on the market today come in clusters or partial hands rather than full bunches as in the past. Most stores sell the fruit on a price-per-pound basis.

An individual banana is called a finger. Its neck is the part attached to the crown. The tip of the banana, usually the last part to lose its green color as the fruit ripens, is the unattached or blossom end.

Buy bananas by the cluster that are not quite full yellow in color. Single bananas have been pulled away from the crown; they are more likely to be bruised or cracked than those in natural groupings.

Buy in relation to menu plans and family eating habits. As an added guide, about two or three medium bananas are in one pound. One pound of unpeeled bananas yields 2 cups sliced or 1½ cups mashed.

How to store: Bananas ripen to full flavor and soft smooth texture very easily at room temperature. To prevent bruises or decay, leave them attached to the crown until ready to use them. When the desired stage of ripening has been reached, bananas can be stored in the refrigerator several days to retard overripening. The skins will darken, but the flavor and texture of the fruit remain unchanged.

How to prepare: The bananas' degree of coloration is a key to how they may best be used. Underripe ones, which appear mostly yellow with a little green on neck and tip, are slightly tart in flavor and have firm, starchy pulp. When baked, broiled, sautéed, or fried, their delicious flavor is enhanced. These underripe fruit are also preferred by some people for out-of-hand eating or for salads.

Broiler Banana Splits

    2 **medium bananas**
      Lemon juice
  ¼ **cup butter or margarine**
  ½ **cup brown sugar**
    2 **tablespoons light cream**
  ½ **cup corn flakes**
      Vanilla ice cream

Peel bananas; split in half lengthwise, then in half crosswise. Place in shallow pan. Brush with lemon juice. In saucepan melt butter; stir in sugar and cream. Cook and stir till bubbly. Remove from heat; add cornflakes. Spoon over bananas.

Broil 5 inches from heat till bubbly (about 2 minutes). Spoon into dishes; top with scoops of ice cream. Makes 4 servings.

Ripe bananas completely yellow in color are ready for any use. Fully ripe bananas have deep yellow peels with brown flecks and are perfect in flavor and texture for eating with cereals, in salads or desserts. These latter bananas can be mashed easily with a fork or rotary beater, or puréed by pushing slices through a strainer.

Banana Ice Cream

  ¾ **cup sugar**
 1½ **teaspoons unflavored gelatin**
  ¾ **cup light cream**
    2 **fully-ripe medium bananas,**
      mashed (1 cup)
    2 **well-beaten egg yolks**
    2 **teaspoons lemon juice**
    1 **teaspoon vanilla**
    2 **cups whipping cream**
    2 **egg whites**

Combine ½ *cup* sugar, gelatin, and ¼ teaspoon salt in saucepan. Stir in light cream. Stir over low heat till gelatin and sugar are dissolved. Chill till partially set.

Blend in banana, yolks, lemon juice, and vanilla. Whip cream; fold into gelatin. Beat egg whites to soft peaks. Gradually add remaining sugar beating to stiff peaks. Fold into banana mixture. Pour into large freezer tray. Freeze firm. Makes 2 quarts.

If cut slices are not to be used immediately, remember to brush the peeled and sliced bananas with ascorbic acid color keeper or lemon juice mixed with a little water to prevent darkening.

How to use: Bananas belong with main dishes as meat accompaniments when glazed or fried; in quick breads, in cakes, cookies, pies, and puddings; in ice cream, sherbet, or other frozen desserts; in milk shakes or nogs; in sauces and toppings; and in salads and some sandwiches. But still most popular of all are the bananas which are peeled and eaten out-of-hand. (See also *Fruit.*)

Strawberry-Banana Mold

    2 3-ounce packages strawberry-
       flavored gelatin
    2 cups boiling water
    1 10-ounce package frozen
       strawberries
    1 cup cold water
            . . .
    2 medium bananas
    1 cup whipping cream

Dissolve gelatin in boiling water. Thaw berries *just enough* to drain off 1 tablespoon syrup; reserve the 1 tablespoon syrup. Add berries to gelatin; break in small chunks with fork then stir to completely thaw berries. Add cold water. Chill till partially set.

Peel bananas. Slice bananas on the bias into gelatin; stir gently to distribute fruit. Pour into 6½-cup fluted mold. Chill till firm; unmold. If desired, garnish with greens and additional bias-cut banana slices dipped in ascorbic acid color keeper to retain color.

Top with *Strawberry Whipped Cream:* Whip cream to soft peaks. Stir reserved strawberry syrup into cream. Makes 8 to 10 servings.

Nut-Crusted Bananas

Peel fully ripe bananas. Cut in half crosswise and then in half lengthwise. Dip in a mixture of equal parts honey and lime juice. Arrange on plate and sprinkle generously with chopped macadamia nuts or walnuts.

Banana Ambrosia Ring

Mix ½ cup flaked coconut; ⅓ cup maple-flavored syrup; and 2 tablespoons butter or margarine, melted. Spread over bottom of 6½-cup ring mold. Combine 2 cups packaged biscuit mix and 3 tablespoons sugar. Stir in 1 banana, mashed (½ cup); 1 slightly beaten egg; and 3 tablespoons butter or margarine, melted.

Beat mixture vigorously for 1 minute. Spoon *half* the batter over coconut in mold. Mix 2 tablespoons sugar with 2 tablespoons butter or margarine, softened, and 1 teaspoon ground cinnamon; sprinkle over batter in mold. Cover with remaining batter. Bake at 375° for 20 minutes or till done. Invert to unmold. Serve warm. Makes 6 to 8 servings.

Banana Fritters

    5 to 6 firm medium bananas
    2 tablespoons orange juice
    1 tablespoon sugar
    1 cup sifted all-purpose flour
    ½ teaspoon baking powder
    ¼ teaspoon salt
    ¾ cup milk
    1 slightly beaten egg
    2 tablespoons butter or margarine,
       melted
    1 teaspoon grated orange peel
    ¼ teaspoon vanilla
       Orange-Lemon Sauce

Peel bananas; cut in 3-inch pieces then halve lengthwise. Let stand in mixture of orange juice and sugar. Sift together flour, baking powder, and salt. Combine next 5 ingredients; add to flour mixture, stirring only till moistened. Drain bananas; dip into batter, spreading batter evenly over bananas.

Fry in deep hot fat (375°) for 2 to 3 minutes or till fritters are golden brown; drain. Serve with whipped cream, if desired. Pass Orange-Lemon Sauce. Makes 6 to 8 servings.

Orange-Lemon Sauce: Combine ½ cup sugar, 1½ tablespoons cornstarch, and dash salt in saucepan; stir in ¾ cup water. Bring mixture to boiling, stirring constantly. Cook and stir till thickened and bubbly. Remove sauce from heat; add ¼ cup orange juice, 2 tablespoons butter or margarine, and 1 tablespoon lemon juice. Serve warm. Makes 1⅓ cups sauce.

Banana Burgers

    1 beaten egg
    ¼ teaspoon ground cinnamon
    1 pound ground beef
    1 small banana
    4 frankfurter buns, split and
        toasted

Combine egg, 1 teaspoon salt, and cinnamon. Add meat; mix well. Peel banana; cut in half crosswise, then in half lengthwise. Divide meat into 4 portions; shape each portion around banana quarter. Broil 3 inches from heat for 12 minutes, turning ¼ turn every 3 minutes. Serve in buns. Makes 4 servings.

Banana Cream Pie

        Plain Pastry for 1-crust 9-inch pie
        (See *Pastry*)
    ¾ cup sugar
    ⅓ cup all-purpose flour *or*
        3 tablespoons cornstarch
    2 cups milk
    3 slightly beaten egg yolks
    2 tablespoons butter or margarine
    1 teaspoon vanilla
    3 ripe medium bananas
        Soft Meringue

Fit rolled Plain Pastry into 9-inch pie plate; flute edges. Prick bottom and sides well with fork. Bake at 450° for 10 to 12 minutes or till golden; cool thoroughly.

Meanwhile, in saucepan combine sugar, flour, and ¼ teaspoon salt; gradually stir in milk. Cook and stir till mixture is thick and bubbly. Cook and stir 2 minutes longer. Remove from heat. Stir small amount of hot mixture into yolks; immediately return to hot mixture. Cook 2 minutes, stirring constantly.

Remove from heat. Add butter and vanilla. Peel bananas; slice into cooled baked pastry shell. Pour pudding over. Spread Soft Meringue on top, sealing to pastry. Bake at 350° about 12 to 15 minutes, or till meringue is golden. Cool pie before cutting.

Soft Meringue: Beat 3 egg whites with ½ teaspoon vanilla and ¼ teaspoon cream of tartar till soft peaks form. Gradually add 6 tablespoons sugar, beating till stiff peaks form and all sugar is dissolved.

Bananas Foster

Peel 6 large ripe bananas and halve lengthwise, brush with lemon juice. In skillet melt ¾ cup brown sugar and 6 tablespoons butter. Add bananas; cook till almost tender, about 3 minutes. Drizzle ¼ cup orange liqueur atop. Serve with ice cream. Makes 6 servings.

Banana Pecan Crunch

    2 tablespoons butter or margarine
    6 medium bananas, peeled and
        sliced crosswise
    ½ cup broken pecans
    2 tablespoons molasses
    ½ cup brown sugar
    2 tablespoons butter or margarine,
        melted

In 11x7x1½-inch baking pan melt the first 2 tablespoons butter; layer bananas and nuts in pan. Drizzle with molasses. Sprinkle brown sugar and melted butter over. Bake at 350° for 10 minutes. Makes 6 servings.

Bubbling Bananas Foster can be an elegant prepare-at-the-table dessert. Serve as is or with scoops of vanilla ice cream.

BANANA FLAKES—Dehydrated, ripe banana in the form of small thin flakes. When rehydrated into mashed banana, banana flakes can be used for infant and invalid feeding. After adding the proper amount of liquid to them, they also can be used as an ingredient in some recipes calling for a specific measure of mashed banana.

BANANA FLOUR—Thoroughly dried, ripe banana finely ground into a nutritious and easily digestible meal. It is white to very pale yellow in color and has a pleasing taste and slightly fruity aroma. Banana flour was designed primarily for use in a semiliquid food served to invalids.

BANANA PEPPER—A slender yellow pepper, usually pickled, that is popular in Italian cuisine as a relish or antipasto ingredient. Banana peppers are primarily marketed in jars and are seldom found fresh on produce counters except in areas where they are grown. (See also *Pepper.*)

BANANA SQUASH—A cylindrical, banana-shaped vegetable of the gourd family. This variety of squash is most frequently served on the Pacific Coast.

In appearance, the outer skin of banana squash is smooth and light greenish-gray to creamy pink in color. Some can grow to a length of 2 feet and weigh 12 pounds. The outer shell is thin and hard. When cooked, the light orange, edible flesh is fine grained, of good flavor, and moderately dry.

Cooking techniques used for banana squash are similar to those used for other winter squash varieties. (See *Squash, Winter Squash* for additional information.)

Baked Banana Squash

```
1 3-pound banana squash
½ cup brown sugar
¼ cup butter or margarine,
    softened
1 teaspoon paprika
```

Cut squash into serving pieces; remove seeds. Place skin side up in baking dish; pour ⅓ cup hot water in dish. Bake 20 minutes at 375°.

Turn squash skin side down. Combine brown sugar, butter, and paprika; spread over squash. Continue baking about 5 to 10 minutes or till squash is tender, basting frequently to glaze. To serve, pass extra butter. Makes 8 servings.

BANBURY TART—A square-, triangular-, round-, or half-moon-shaped pastry with a tart-sweet filling of raisins and currants. These pies in miniature were named after the city of Banbury, England. The name is sometimes given to short, filled cookies or bars with similar filling. (See *English Cookery, Tart* for additional information.)

Banbury Tarts

```
¼ cup sugar
1 teaspoon cornstarch
¼ teaspoon ground cinnamon
¼ teaspoon ground nutmeg
½ cup water
1 teaspoon grated lemon peel
1 tablespoon lemon juice
1 cup raisins
  Plain Pastry for 2-crust 9-inch
    pie (See *Pastry*)
  Milk *or* egg yolk
```

In saucepan, blend sugar, cornstarch, cinnamon, and nutmeg. Stir in water, lemon peel and juice; add raisins. Cook and stir till thickened and bubbly; cool.

Cut rolled Plain Pastry into twelve 5-inch circles. Place about 1 tablespoon raisin mixture on half of each pastry round. Moisten edges; fold over and press together with a fork. Brush with milk or slightly beaten egg yolk. Cut slit in top to permit steam to escape. Place tarts on cookie sheet. Bake at 350° for 25 to 30 minutes or till browned.

BANNOCK *(ban' uhk)*—An oatmeal, wheat meal, or barley hearth bread popular in Scotland and England. Modern-day bannocks are usually baked on a griddle instead of before open hearths or fires as was done in years past. The Scottish people serve bannocks as frequently as biscuits are served in the southern United States. (See also *English Cookery.*)